Fight
or
Flight

The Ultimate Book for Understanding
and Managing Stress

Gary R. Plaford, M.S.W., L.C.S.W.

Fight or Flight
The Ultimate Book for Understanding and Managing Stress
Copyright © 2018 by Gary R. Plaford

Library of Congress Control Number: 2018933613
ISBN-13:   Paperback: 978-1-64151-476-7

Printed in the United States of America

LitFire
PUBLISHING

LitFire LLC
1-800-511-9787
www.litfirepublishing.com
order@litfirepublishing.com

CONTENTS

PART I

Understanding Stress

Introduction

Albert Einstein once said, "The most important question any human being can ask themselves is, 'Is this a friendly universe?'" I believe we each need to ask ourselves that very question, "Is this a friendly universe for me?" If it is not, it will bring a great deal of stress. The interesting thing is that the answer to that question is to a great extent based on the way we think, the thoughts we have, the thought patterns we choose, and the way we choose to look at and interpret our very own universe.

Stress is an integral part of our lives. We face stress in varying amounts almost every day of our lives. Some stresses are mild, some are in the moderate range, and some stresses are very intense. These stresses come in many forms. Some of the stress we face is physical, some of it is emotional, some of it is mental, and some of it is spiritual. The spiritual includes religion and religious beliefs, but it encompasses much more.

Besides the fact that we face stress in many forms and in multiple degrees, we need to understand that all stress isn't necessarily bad. In fact, it is often stress that motivates us to act. Stress can motivate us to create. Stress can motivate us to make decisions. Stress can motivate us to improve ourselves in a variety of ways or improve our situations. On the other hand, stress at its most intense levels creates a fight or flight response. This response is designed to save us. True, it sometimes gets in the way and causes us to not function at the level we want, but it is designed to save our lives in times of real danger, and it can do so.

When we think about stress we typically think about managing stress. There are multiple resources out there that give different strategies for doing just that. To manage stress effectively, however, we must first make an effort to really understand stress. This means understanding the purpose of stress, understanding the conditions that create stress, understanding what happens in the body when we experience stress, understanding a little about brain functioning and the locus of control and how this is interconnected with stress, understanding a little about mind set and habitual thought patterns in relation to stress, and finally understanding how the level of stress we are facing may affect each of us differently.

Once we have a better understanding of the nature of stress in our lives, then we can move on to managing stress more effectively. Managing stress effectively means managing stress as it relates to all the facets of our lives. This means what we can do to manage stress physically, mentally, emotionally, and spiritually. Stress encompasses all of these realms of our life, so to manage stress effectively we need to have strategies to address it in some manner in each of these realms.

This book is divided into two parts. The first part is focused on understanding stress. In these chapters we discuss the role of stress in our lives, stress and emotional intelligence, the conditions that cause stress, how the brain works when stressed, stress and mindset, and finally stress and automatic thought patterns. The second part of the book focusses on how we go about managing stress.

CHAPTER 1

A Primer on Stress

Many people think and feel by default. Their thoughts and their feelings are on autopilot. They believe that whatever thoughts they think and whatever feelings they feel are destined to be. That is simply not true, or rather it does not need to be true. The old saying, "When life gives you lemons make lemonade" sounds nice and optimistic on a behavioral level. However, that saying is profoundly true at a much deeper level. We make that lemonade with our thoughts. We cannot make lemonade out of lemons with our actions until we have first done so with our thoughts and our thought patterns. The Chinese symbol for "crisis" is really a combination of two other symbols, one for "danger" and the other for "opportunity." We can make lemonade out of a crisis only if we focus on the opportunity beyond the danger, only when we can get past our stress.

When I speak at conferences about stress I usually begin with a short story, joke, or observation. One I have often used is to ask the audience to use their imaginations with me for a moment, and to imagine that I am holding a glass that is filled to about the halfway point with water. When we imagine that, some people will imagine a glass that is half full...optimistic. Some will imagine a glass that is half empty...pessimistic. Some will imagine that the glass is merely too big, if it were smaller it would be full... pragmatic possibly. Some will even imagine that the glass is dirty and needs to be washed... Obsessive Compulsive Disorder or OCD. I'm sure my wife thinks I have OCD because I think like this. I'm sure I do not have OCD, but if I did have OCD I would not call it OCD, I would call it CDO, because that is in alphabetical order as things are supposed to be. My point is, even when we think of something as simple as a glass of water people can and do have different perspectives. When we think about something as complex as stress, people certainly do have different thoughts and perspectives. My goal is first of all to provide some perspectives that might be new, and thus some strategies for managing stress that might be both new and effective.

Dr. Daniel Amen, in his children's book, *Mind Coach,* begins by talking about polygraph testing, or lie detectors. What do they really measure? They do not measure lies, but rather they measure a stress response. Typical lie detector tests have looked at such things as hand temperature, heart rate, blood pressure, breathing rate, muscle tension, and perspiration.

When we are under stress the temperature in our hands drops. Why? Because under stress blood flow begins to divert to the major muscle groups for possible fight or flight. Hence the hands and feet get less blood and less oxygen, and the temperature in the hands and feet drops. Have you ever been stressed, anxious, or frightened and tried to do something that took some dexterity and you felt like you were all thumbs? Something like trying to get a key into a lock or open a combination lock? Part of the issue may be lack of focus of concentration on the task at hand, but part of it is that our hands are getting less blood and oxygen at that point. Our fingers aren't working as well as they do when we are not stressed.

Heart rate also increases under stress. Have you noticed that under stress your heart is beating faster, your pulse quickens, you feel a throbbing in your temple? This is because your body is preparing for the fight or flight mode, and your major muscles require more blood and oxygen if you have to fight or flee.

Additionally, because of the accelerated blood flow your blood pressure increases. Blood, and hence oxygen, are flowing less to the extremities which means there is a buildup of blood in the major arteries to carry the extra oxygen the major muscles might need.

Breathing rate also increases. If you notice, while under pressure, the number of breaths you take per minute escalates. Again, this is because the muscles require more oxygen during fight or flight so the lungs must take in more oxygen and pump more oxygen.

Muscles also will tense up and tighten up under stress. When we have been under stress and finally notice that our neck is all tensed up or our back is in a knot, this is due to the tensing of the muscles in preparation for fight or flight.

Finally, under pressure we will begin to perspire more. When the lungs work harder at breathing, and the heart works harder at getting that oxygen to the muscles via blood flow, then the body is simply working harder, and the body temperature rises. By sweating the body is attempting to cool itself off.

The opposite of a stress response is relaxation. When we relax the hands become a little warmer, the heart rate slows sown, blood pressure goes down, the breathing rate slows, the muscles relax, and the perspiration dries up.

The point is that when we experience stress it is these physical responses we are having that a lie detector is actually detecting. It is not detecting lies, it is detecting a stress response. It is also interesting that when we talk to someone who is under stress and the words coming out of their mouth do not match what we are seeing in their physical responses, the truth always lies in the physical responses as opposed to their words. The reason is that it is fairly easy for most people to lie with their words, but it is very difficult to mask the physical responses they are having. When someone says "No, I'm not angry," but their teeth are clenched, their jaw is set, their arms are crossed defiantly across their chest, their posture is not open but rather turned away from us, the truth of what they are really feeling is in the physical response. People can obviously be trained to mask their physical responses, but that is fairly rare.

What happens in the body when we experience a stress response? The first thing that happens is that cortisol production increases. Cortisol is often called the stress hormone. Cortisol will then give rise to adrenaline, epinephrine and nor-epinephrine. The body is then peaked for action of some kind. This is why we sometimes will see feats of super human strength as a mother lifts an automobile off her child to save the child.

Another occurrence under stress is that levels of serotonin diminish. Serotonin is a neurotransmitter that soothes us, that calms us, that gives us peace. An interesting aside is that when physicians prescribe Prozac for individuals who are clinically depressed, one of the desired results is an increase in serotonin levels. Prozac does not actually increase the level of serotonin, but rather it keeps the serotonin the body produces in the synapses longer, thus having a calming effect. In other words, Prozac is a serotonin reuptake inhibitor. Because Prozac does not actually cause the body to produce more serotonin but merely keeps it in play longer, if an individual is not producing enough serotonin in the first place, then Prozac will not have the intended result. This is why some people who take Prozac will have a different response from that which was intended.

The result of these physical reactions to stress, having more cortisol in the system and less serotonin, is that the body is now primed for fight or flight. The fight or flight response is a normal, natural response. We need this response. It is designed to protect us, to save us. For example, say we are taking a walk in the woods and see a snake. The automatic response is to jump back. Notice at this point in time breathing is accelerated and the pulse is racing. We are primed for fight or flight. In this case we have already experienced a little flight, we jumped back, but we are physically ready for more action if necessary. Then, as we watch the snake, we realize it has not moved. We watch a little longer and realize it is not a snake after all, it is a stick. Now we may feel silly, but the point is our fight of flight response kicked in to save us. That could have been a snake. Next time it might be a snake. Our limbic system, which is a set of deep brain structures that deal with multiple issues including emotions, and specifically the amygdala which is what triggers the fight or flight response, does not wait for the neo-cortex to figure out all the clues to whether it is a snake or not before reacting. If it did we might be dead. It responds, and it responds quickly to danger or the threat of danger. It is a defense mechanism designed to protect us. True, it sometimes gets in our way and we cannot shut it off as we would like, but it is designed for our safety. In fact, when we are in fight or flight, the locus of control for brain functioning actually shifts to the limbic system. Joseph LeDoux refers to the limbic system as the emotional system because calling it the limbic system may be misleading and it may actually be more than one system, but the point is the locus of control is there rather than in the right or left hemisphere. When the locus of control is in the limbic system we are less able to focus on conversation, we are less able to attend to other things in our surroundings, we cannot really pay attention to what someone is saying because we are focused on survival. We are watching for danger cues.

There have been numerous studies with rats, monkeys, and other animals concerning the role of the amygdala in initiating fear and the fight or flight response. Researchers like Joseph LeDoux and J. L. Downer have studied the implications when the amygdala is damaged, impeded, or removed from such animals. Rats, for example, normally fear a cat and will respond accordingly when a cat is in close proximity. In fact they will send out a noise to other rats, which cannot be heard by the human ear, that signals the proximity of danger. However, if a rat had its amygdala removed it would not fear a cat, and the fight or flight response would not be initiated. In that situation the rat would be in grave danger of being killed because the fight or flight response did not kick in as it should have. The fight or flight response is definitely designed to give us stress when facing potentially dangerous situations and cause us to react accordingly. When it does not kick in, for whatever reason, there are often problems.

Another problem occurs when this response kicks in and stays kicked in long term. When we experience long, ongoing periods of high stress the body stays keyed up in all the ways previously mentioned, and a few more that are more subtle. For one thing cortisol suppresses the immune response and acts as an anti-inflammatory agent. High levels of cortisol over an extended period of time can make us ill because the body isn't allowed to fight off bacteria, viruses, or tumor cells as it is designed to do.

Another result of high levels of cortisol over extended periods is that cortisol actually erodes or depletes the hippocampus. The hippocampus is part of the limbic system in the brain. The hippocampus is important in memory consolidation, and in managing emotions like stress. Dr. Sonjia Lupine has done some interesting research with patients suffering from Post-Traumatic Stress Disorder. One of the issues these patients face is that the hippocampus is smaller than it should be. It has been depleted or shrunken due to the continuous high levels of cortisol in these individuals. In some cases is was probably the stress event itself (like being in a war zone and being shot at every day for long periods of time) that caused the high, prolonged levels of cortisol and resulted in the shrinking of the hippocampus. In some cases it was probably that the patient already had a depleted or shrunken hippocampus, and when put in a high stress situation the brain could not manage the added stress which resulted in the Post-Traumatic Stress response. The reason we know that is because Dr. Lupine also studied siblings of PTSD patients. These siblings did not have PTSD, yet some of them did have a shrunken hippocampus. When social histories were taken of these siblings who had a shrunken hippocampus it was learned that the PTSD patient and their sibling grew up in environments where they faced high levels of stress during childhood. Hence, they were pre-programed for PTSD if and when they faced highly stressful events in life.

Additionally, when we experience a fight or flight response the sympathetic nervous system response kicks in and cortisol, adrenaline, epinephrine, and nor-epinephrine are produced. Later the parasympathetic nervous system response kicks in and we relax. The sympathetic response is like pressing the accelerator on a car and we go faster. The parasympathetic response is like pressing on the brake, we slow down. Sometimes, however, the parasympathetic response does not kick in, and sometimes we experience what is termed a "freeze" response.

We have seen the freeze response in movies. An example would be in horror movies when the monster comes around the corner and a woman is standing there, sees the monster, but does nothing. She does not run. She does not scream. She just stands there with a look of horror on her face until the monster approaches her and kills her. The audience is usually screaming for her to run or scream or do something, but to no avail. We often think that is stupid, but in reality it can happen. She has had a freeze response. We think of this commonly as "the deer in the headlights" response.

A freeze response happens in nature, not merely with humans. There are instances when an animal is suddenly confronted by a snake and the animal just freezes. I have heard people try to explain the behavior by saying the snake hypnotized the animal. In reality, the animal had a freeze response. Sometimes in the wild it has been observed that a predator chases down its prey, and when the prey is finally cornered it will have a freeze response. It stops running, it stands there, and sometimes it will even fall over. What is happening is that the animal perceives that death in imminent, that there is nothing more to do. Hence the animal produces endorphins to make the pain of death less intense.

When this occurs in nature sometimes the predator will strike a killing blow and feast, but sometimes it will not. If the predator has cubs, sometimes it will go back for the cubs to bring them to the feast never having struck a killing blow. When this occurs, if the cubs are far enough away, the prey has time to recover from all the bio-chemicals in its system. This includes the cortisol, the adrenaline, the epinephrine, and nor-epinephrine of the fight or flight response, as well as the endorphins from the freeze response. While it is recovering is shudders and shakes violently, it takes in a series of deep breaths, it sweats, and it shakes off the effects of these bio-chemicals. The predator is probably quite surprised when it returns to find no prey there, but that is nature for you.

In humans, when we experience a freeze response, several things happen somewhat differently. First of all, we tend not to shudder and shake enough to throw off the effects of the bio-chemicals. When we see someone after a traumatic event and they are shaking we typically try to stop it. We hold them, we cover them with blankets, etc. There is certainly the fear of someone going into shock, and that is a real concern. However, when we don't throw off the effect of all these bio-chemicals the parasympathetic system does not kick in, we do not return to a baseline, the over-charged sympathetic system stays keyed up and it becomes self-perpetuating. This is called kindling. The alarm stays on.

Dissociation may well be a part of the freeze response. Dissociation is when we disconnect from our sensations and emotions. We see this sometimes after a bad automobile accident. An individual in the accident thought they were going to die, but they somehow survived and walked away. When we talk to this person they sometimes describe the accident as though they were watching it instead of being a part of it. They state that it was like they were floating above it, detached from it, watching what was happening. That is mental distancing from the event. It is dissociation from the pain of the event and from the thought of eminent death from the event. Dissociation is both a key element of PTSD and a key predictor of PTSD.

A second thing that happens with humans after a freeze response is that we attach negative meaning to the immobility, to the fact that we froze in the face of danger. We think we were cowardly, weak-willed, incompetent or soiled in some intrinsic manner. We beat ourselves up with guilt.

I am reminded of a conversation I once had with a good friend. I was explaining some things about fight or flight and the freeze response when she suddenly said, "That's it." I asked, "That's what?" She then related an incident that happened when her two sons were very young. A relevant fact here is that she was a non-swimmer. She was not only a non-swimmer, she was terrified of the water. None-the-less, one afternoon she took her sons down to a lake and out onto a pier. One of her sons fell into the water and she just stood there. He was drowning and she could do nothing but watch. She didn't attempt to save him or to scream for help, she merely watched. A nearby stranger saw what was happening, ran out onto the pier, jumped into the water and saved her son. She was incredibly grateful, but also very distraught. She could not understand her own inaction. She felt she must be a terrible person, a horrible parent. How could she do nothing when her son was in jeopardy? All her life she had suffered with these thoughts. When she said, "That's it," it was because she suddenly understood what had happened to her. She had experienced a freeze response. All these years she had emotionally beaten herself up because of a response over which she really had no control.

The fight or flight response and the freeze response are normal responses that we sometimes have when we experience very high levels of stress. Often this happens with children. What can cause high levels of stress, and hence high and prolonged levels of cortisol, in childhood? A number of things could be the cause. Growing up with abuse on a regular basis could do it. Being hit, slapped, burnt or otherwise mistreated on a regular basis by those who are supposed to protect you, and never knowing when it will happen is stressful. Growing up with neglect could also result in high stress. Not knowing if there will be food to eat the next day, or if there will be a roof over your head, or heat so you can stay warm can create high anxiety. Witnessing domestic violence could also bring about stress. Watching your mother being beaten up by your father, or boyfriend, or series of boyfriends on a regular basis is stressful. Being bullied regularly at school is also stressful. Bullying typically occurs at school, not because schools promote bullying but because this is where children congregate, and hence this is where we most need to address bullying. Now, with the growth of cyber bullying, bullying happens more than merely at school, but it is still most often at school where bullies find their victims. Growing up in poverty can also create high levels of stress. Moving around regularly, not knowing where your next meal is coming from, not having any control over your life, and feeling that you somehow do not measure up are all contributors to high stress levels.

This is a huge reason why dealing with issues like abuse and neglect, domestic violence, bullying, and the overwhelming issues of poverty are critical for our society. The issues themselves are important, but it is also what they do to children relative to stress and setting them up to not be capable of effectively managing stress the rest of their lives that is of utmost importance.

Another issue related to stress is the impact stress has in decision making. Some very interesting research was done which resulted in what is now referred to most often as the Iowa Gambling Task. This was originally developed to help determine decision-making problems in patients with damage to the prefrontal cortex. It is now used widely to look at decision-making. The task is this; there are four decks of cards from which subjects can draw. The subjects are told to earn or win as much money as they can. The cards they select will state that they win a certain amount of money, or sometimes that they lose a certain amount of money. Subjects can select cards from any of the four decks in any order they choose. What they are not told is that the decks are rigged. There are two "good" decks and two "bad" decks. Basically what that means is that if the subject selects mostly from the "good" decks he will win. The winnings will be smaller, but the losses will also be smaller, and overall the subject will come out well ahead. The "bad" decks, on the other hand, have greater winnings but also greater losses, and selecting from those will guarantee ultimate losses. The subject learns this by trial and error.

The interesting outcome of this task is that after about fifty cards an individual, without brain impairment, will begin to alter their decisions about which decks to draw from. They will begin to draw mostly from the two decks where they are winning the most, the "good" decks. When asked why they were drawing mostly from these two decks they could not explain their behavior, they did not rationally know why they were doing that. At about eighty cards the intellect kicks in. Now they can state why they are drawing from the "good" decks...they are winning more consistently from those. Rationality has kicked in. The really interesting thing is, when subjects are hooked up to machines to determine their stress response during the task, they begin having a stress response when they select cards from the "bad" decks after about only ten cards.

What is this telling us? After ten cards a stress response was kicking in, the subjects felt stress when they chose from the "bad" decks. At around fifty cards their behavior was changing, now they were drawing mostly from the "good" decks and avoiding the "bad" decks but they could not state why. After about eighty cards their intellect kicked in, now they knew what was happening and could act on it rationally. The point is that stress was giving them information. The body knows at some base level, at an emotional stress level, that something is wrong with the "bad" decks. Our stress level does give us valuable information and it can definitely help us make decisions if used wisely. Unfortunately at times it can also get in the way of healthy, wise decisions.

Another example of this comes from United States military operations in 1991. Jonah Lehrer gives an account of this in his book, *How We Decide.* Iraq had fortified military positions in Kuwait and the U. S. military went into action. A part of this operation included support from naval ships off shore. The ships were close enough to shore that they could be threatened by Iraqi missiles. At 5:01 one morning Lieutenant Commander Michael Riley was watching his radar screen and noticed a blip coming at their ship. The blip could have been a missile, but it could also have been a naval fighter returning from the operation. The blip was traveling at the same speed and same altitude as a friendly fighter, so it could have been a fighter, but for some reason it made him nervous. He felt stress as he watched the fast moving blip for about a minute. The blip was moving toward the U.S. naval ship at over 550 miles per hour, so if he was going to shoot it down he needed to do so quickly. He had watched other blips and not felt so stressed, but something about this one was kicking up his stress level. He made the decision to shoot it down. Immediately his commanding officer asked him what he had just shot down, and Lieutenant Commander Riley stated he was not completely sure. They went into action to both send rescue helicopters if it had been a friendly fighter, and took measures to try to account for all friendly fighters. Eventually it was determined that the blip had been in fact an Iraqi missile, and Lieutenant Commander Riley had saved the ship from a missile strike.

Then the really interesting part happened. They tried to determine how Lieutenant Commander Riley had made his decision. How did he determine it was a missile and not a friendly fighter? What had made him feel stressed over this blip? It was traveling at the same speed as a fighter, and at the same altitude. What they finally determined was that this blip had appeared on the radar screen later than it would have if it had been a fighter. If it had been a fighter it would have been at the same altitude for a longer time. A missile, on the other hand, had to climb from ground level to that altitude before it could be picked up by radar. Lieutenant Commander Riley was not cognitively aware of this detail in his thinking, but on a gut level he knew something was wrong, and he shot the blip/missile down.

The interesting thing to understand here is that emotions, specifically stressful emotions, do give us information. There is a reason we don't feel good about something, why it makes us nervous. Sometimes we cannot rationally, cognitively put our finger on it, but for some reason it just doesn't feel right. It is like the tenth card in the Iowa Gambling Task, our gut is telling us there is a problem but it won't be until much later that our intellect figures out exactly what the problem is.

Another issue in this emotional/stress related aspect of decision making is that our decisions are based on predictions. We make predictions based on expectations, and when we are surprised, as when our expectations are not met or not met in the manner we predicted, then we both react to that and we learn from that. Our reactions are to a great degree influenced by dopamine release. Wolfram Schultz studied this issue of dopamine release in monkeys several decades ago. His studies mimicked those of Pavlov with his dogs years before. Schultz would sound a loud tone, wait a few seconds, then give a taste of apple juice as a reward. What he found was that after the loud tone but before the apple juice was given, dopamine would be released in the monkey's brain. The monkey had learned to expect the reward, the apple juice. Once the apple juice was received by the monkey even more dopamine was released in the brain, it was pleasurable. However, when the loud tone was sounded and no juice was given, the monkeys would become upset because the prediction of apple juice was wrong. Dopamine release was subsequently diminished because the expectations of juice were not met. The cortex, the thinking part of the brain, takes notice rapidly when such predictions and expectations are not met. Nothing focuses our attention as quickly as surprise.

Another part of this study was that sometimes the juice was given without the preceding loud tone. It was a positive surprise. The release of dopamine when this occurred was even greater than the release for the expected juice reward. In other words, when surprise occurs we really sit up and take notice because this is new information that could be critical. Again surprise, whether negative or positive, really focuses our attention. When that surprise is stress provoking, as when something is happening and we do not comprehend it, like Lieutenant Commander Riley seeing a blip on the radar, then we really take notice and we take notice quickly.

Why does the focus of our attention happen so rapidly? Human beings and great apes have what are called spindle cells. These spindle cells are long and narrow, unlike most other brain cells. They transmit electrical impulses faster than any other neurons. What this accomplishes is that these cells insure that the entire cortex is immediately experiencing the same emotion. These spindle cells are found only in humans and great apes which indicates that the evolution of these spindle cells goes along with higher cognition. In other words, the ability to experience emotions, positive or negative, and have them interwoven with our decision making capabilities is an advancement in evolution.

Emotions impacting our decision making is not a negative thing, but rather an advancement. Emotions, positive or negative, stress producing or stress reducing, help us make the tough decisions in our complicated lives.

Basically, the role of stress in our lives is one of protection. Stress, and all that comes along with it, is designed to protect us. If we heed that stress it also provides us with information that helps us make decisions. On the other hand, too much stress over too long a period of time can be very detrimental to both our ability to function and to our physical, mental, and emotional well-being.

In Summation

1. When we experience stress we have physiological reactions that are measurable; the temperature in the extremities drops because blood flow is being diverted, the heart rate accelerates, blood pressure increases, breathing rate goes up, muscles tense up, and we perspire more.

2. A relaxation response has just the opposite effect.

3. Under stress cortisol production increases and serotonin production decreases priming us for fight or flight.

4. The fight or flight response is designed as a defense mechanism to protect us in times of danger.

5. When we remain in the fight of flight response long term there are problems such as a deterioration of the hippocampus.

6. Additionally, when the sympathetic nervous response does not turn off and the parasympathetic response does not kick in, we can experience a freeze response.

7. Dissociation is presumed to be part of the freeze response.

8. High levels of stress in childhood decrease our ability to manage stress the rest of our lives. High levels of stress in childhood can be caused by such ongoing events as abuse, neglect, domestic violence, bullying, or poverty.

9. Stress impacts decision making. While it can sometimes be a detriment to decision making, stress often gives us information important in decision making.

10. Decisions are based on predictions. We feel rewarded when our predictions are correct, but we pay very close attention whenever we are surprised because that is potentially new and important information.

11. The emotions we experience as humans, and the stress that comes with these emotions, are an advancement in evolution not a relic from a more primitive past.

12. Stress serves as a protective function, but too much for too long can be very detrimental.

CHAPTER 2

Stress and Emotional Intelligence

An airplane takes off most effectively into the wind. As the plane taxis down the runway and picks up speed the wind pushes against the wings and lifts the plane into the air. It is in part the resistance that lifts the plane up. Likewise, in life, it is what we push against that lifts us up...the resistance, the obstacles, the opposition, the discouragement, the disappointment, the stressors that we overcome. It is overcoming the resistance that we face in life that ultimately allows us to soar.

Now that we have discussed a little about the purpose of stress, it is time to consider the difference in levels of stress. Some people talk about stress as if it were always and totally a bad thing. It is not. It can be, certainly. But it is not always bad. Besides the negative aspects of stress, stress can be motivational and can lead us to great accomplishments. What is the difference? Why does it sometimes cause us significant problems and at other times results in very positive outcomes? One of the reasons is due to the level of stress we are experiencing.

For the purposes of discussion, let's talk about stress as though it occurred as specific measurable points or levels as opposed to on a continuum. In reality, of course, it is better described as a continuum. But if we thought about it in levels there would be the level of no stress, there would be mild stress, there would be moderate stress, and there would be high stress.

The "no stress" level would be a state where we were experiencing absolutely no stress. This is like being in a hammock on a very nice beach. The temperature is perfect, there is a gentle breeze off the ocean, the hammock we are in is resting in the shade of a huge palm tree, there is soft music in the background, and there is a pleasant drink by our side. We are experiencing no stress and we are not inclined to do anything but enjoy it.

Mild stress would be a state where we are experiencing just a little stress. In the beach example possibly a little sand gets into the hammock, or the sun has moved around the side of the palm tree and is now in our eyes. So what do we do? Now we take action. We get up and shake out the hammock to get the sand out and we pull the hammock around to the other side of the tree so we are again out of the sun. The point is, the mild stress causes us to act, to do something to relieve the stress.

Say we are experiencing mild stress at work. Possibly we are having some difficulties with a fellow employee. What do we do? We may decide to try to talk it out with our fellow worker. We may try to buy them a cup of coffee and sit down for a heart to heart talk. We may decide to talk to the supervisor about the issue to get their input and help. We may decide to just try to avoid that person for a while until whatever issue exists goes away. We may also talk to other employees to get their suggestions or advice. Or we may decide that we need to change something about how we are functioning or acting at work because that may be the problem. The point is we are doing something to address the stress.

In education, teachers create mild stress for students on a regular basis by assigning homework or by announcing on Monday that there will be a test on Friday. This creates enough mild stress in most students that they will do something, they will act. The action is typically to do the homework assignment or to study for the upcoming test. If they know the material, that reduces the stress. In fact, that is typically why students study. Most students don't study the material because they really just want to know it, they study to relieve the stress they are experiencing due to the upcoming test and the negative results if they don't pass the test.

Mild stress causes us to act. It causes us to achieve. It causes us to look at what is stressing us and make a decision on how to address that issue.

High Stress

(We're in Fight or Flight)

Moderate Stress

(We Take Action)

Mild Stress

(We Take Action)

No Stress

(We Do Nothing/Comfort Zone)

Moderate stress is a little more of the same except the stakes are higher. The potential negative or positive outcomes are a little more important. Or the end results are potentially more open to public scrutiny...we could be embarrassed because whatever happens will be known by everyone. The decisions made and the tasks taken on under moderate stress may seem more daunting but we still typically will make decisions and take action.

High stress can be a different animal entirely. With no stress we do nothing, with mild or moderate stress we take action to resolve the stress, but with high stress we are primed for fight or flight. We flee to protect ourselves, or we fight to protect ourselves. Under high stress we are not interested in taking action to resolve the stress, we are interested in taking action to get away from the stress or protect ourselves from the stress.

With the beach example, high stress might occur if the temperature has risen to an unbearable stage even in the shade, or the gentle breeze has become a gust that is unbearable. In either event we get up and go inside, we flee the elements.

At school the child who is experiencing high stress because of the upcoming test won't be there on Friday. He will be truant, or he will be faking illness at home or in the nurse's office. He will be anywhere else he can be to flee from taking the test.

What happens when we experience high stress at work on a daily basis? Rather than figuring out how to resolve the stress, we more often start looking at getting another job. That can be difficult if we feel somewhat trapped in the job, but quite often we start thinking about how long we can take it, what else we could do, we might search the want ads or start talking to contacts, etc. The point is, now we are not focused on resolving the issue or issues that are stressing us, we are looking instead about fleeing the situation, getting away from the stress.

Mild or moderate stress cause us to try to resolve issues, high stress causes us to run from issues. If we face high stress on a regular basis we begin to learn patterns of running away instead of patterns of decision making and problem solving. This is an important distinction. If we learn patterns or habits of running away from things that stress us, then any time we become stressed our first instinct is to run.

Earlier I mentioned that growing up in poverty creates high levels of stress. I will discuss why that occurs a little later, but the fact is, it does. Because of these constant high stress levels, children growing up in poverty learn patterns of running from problems rather than facing and resolving problems. One of the ultimate outcomes of this affects relationships. How many households in poverty are single parent households? If people have learned patterns of running from stressful situations, then whenever stress pops up in a relationship one of the partners will basically say, "I'm outa here." Is this really so surprising if the basic pattern one has learned is to run or flee from issues?

When therapists or counselors work with people about stress and stress management, a key then is not to eliminate stress but rather to lower it to a manageable level. If you completely take away the individual's stress then they have no incentive to act, to make decisions, to do anything. It is like they are now in that comfortable hammock on the beach. When we don't remove the stress but merely lower it, now the individual will still have the motivation to act but will not be so overwhelmed that they want to flee. Now they can actually focus on what steps might actually solve or resolve the issue.

What determines, in any situation, whether we experience mild, moderate, or high stress? After all, what causes high stress in one person will only cause mild stress in another. Hence, it is not always the situation that causes us stress, but rather what goes on inside us. One critical factor that helps to determine the level of stress we feel is the level of our emotional intelligence. Daniel Goleman, in his book *Emotional Intelligence,* states that there are five domains of emotional intelligence.

The first domain is that of understanding or recognizing one's own emotions, or having self-awareness. This means having the ability to recognize what we are feeling when we are feeling it. An inability to recognize what we are feeling when we are feeling it leaves us at the mercy of those feelings. There is no way to control or manage any emotion unless we can recognize that emotion when it is occurring.

Another part of recognizing emotions is to have a wide range of emotions to recognize. Some children, and unfortunately some adolescents and even some adults have a very limited range of recognizable emotions. They do not recognize much beyond the basic emotions of mad, glad, or sad. If that is the limit for what we know, what we can recognize, then how can we possibly express emotions like disappointment or frustration. If we feel frustrated,

Gary R. Plaford

for example, but we can only express what we are feeling as either mad or sad, then we cannot really do a good job of explaining our feelings to someone else. Not only can we not explain what we are feeling well to others, but we will also have more trouble dealing with or managing that frustration. Strategies in managing frustration are considerably different from strategies for managing either anger or sadness.

Take it one step further. If we cannot recognize that we are feeling frustration, as opposed to being mad or sad, then how can we recognize frustration in someone else? The fact is, we cannot. If we cannot recognize frustration in the first place, then we cannot recognize it in others, which means we will never be capable of feeling empathy for someone else who is feeling frustration. The very basis for empathy is all about the recognition of emotions. A great example of this is bullying. Bullies often do not recognize the emotions of their victims and therefore feel no empathy for them. This is especially true with cyber bullying because cyber bullying is done from a distance, we don't see the victim face to face during the bullying event, and therefore it is very easy to not feel empathy for them. The bottom line is that the recognition of emotions is the very first step, or first domain of building emotional intelligence.

There was an interesting study done by Peter Gordon, a behavioral scientist at Columbia University. He studied the Piraha tribe of Indians who live along the Amazon River in Brazil. He studied them because they have a very limited vocabulary regarding counting. They have one word that means roughly one, another word that means a small quantity, and another word that means many. That is their numerical vocabulary. They do not have words for integers...one, two, three, four, etc. Therefore, if we gave one of these tribal members a bag of apples and asked him to divide them equally between himself and another person, he would not count them out. He would arrange them in two separate piles that look about the same. He would not go through any kind of counting, "one for you, one for me," kind of procedure. He would not do that because he has no ability to conceptualize it in that manner because he has no words for it. It is not impossible nceptualize ideas without words, but it is very difficult. When we come up with new concepts in science, for example, the first inklings of the new concepts may be formed without words, but then we create words quickly so we can better conceptualize and explain the new concept. Having language for something is critical for being able to conceptualize an idea and truly comprehend that idea. The same is true with emotional language. If we do not have the language for frustration, then we really will have trouble recognizing and expressing what it is we are feeling.

The second domain of emotional intelligence is managing one's emotions. This involves the ability to soothe oneself, to shake off anxiety, gloom, and irritability, to overcome the consequences of failure. We all fail, and we fail quite often. Thomas Edison invented the practical, usable version of the light bulb as we know it. But Thomas Edison tested thousands of filaments before he developed one that was both durable and practical. Some people would say that he failed thousands of times before he was successful. But Thomas Edison said, "Results, I have gotten results. If I find 10,000 ways something won't work I haven't failed because every wrong attempt is a step forward." Success is not about not failing, it is about getting back up and trying again. When we learn to ice skate we fall down a lot. Each time we fall, that is failure. But learning to ice skate is about getting back up and trying again. If we can get back up one more time than we fall, we will eventually learn to ice skate.

Managing emotions is the same thing. If we give up in the face of failure, depression, anxiety, gloom, or anger we will be doomed to not learn the lessons of success, of overcoming, of triumph. Managing emotions is all about this overcoming. It does not mean that we can control the emotions that come into our lives. Life happens. Bad things at times happen. It does mean that we have some say in how long certain emotions remain with us. When we lose someone important to us we will certainly grieve that loss, but eventually we must move on with life. Moving on does not mean forgetting, it means healing. This is part of managing our emotions. If we cannot do that we are doomed to eternal grief.

We will forever be caught in the tumult of a raging emotional sea. Talk about stress!

The Five Domains of Emotional Intelligence

Knowing/recognizing one's own emotions...as one feels them

Managing one's emotions...soothing oneself, overcoming failure

Motivating oneself...delaying gratification, stifling impulses

Recognizing the emotions of others...the ability to feel empathy

Managing relationships...the ability to manage the emotions of others, being able to listen, share, or take turns

---

The third domain of emotional intelligence is the ability to motivate oneself, which involves controlling impulses and delaying gratification. To focus our emotions to achieve a goal is essential for paying attention, for self-motivation, for mastery of any skill, and for creativity. The ability to stifle impulses, to delay gratification underlies all accomplishment.

Walter Mischel, a psychologist at Stanford University, conducted a longitudinal study involving delayed gratification. He began with four year old children. First he tested each child to determine his/her I.Q. score. Then he spent some time talking with each child. After a while he stated that he had to leave for a short time but would return. He placed a marshmallow in front of each child and stated that this was a thank you for participating in this study and talking to him. He told the child that they could eat the marshmallow any time they chose, but if they could wait until

---

he returned before eating the marshmallow then they would get a second marshmallow. They did not have to wait, that was entirely their choice. This marshmallow was theirs regardless, but they would only get a second marshmallow if they waited for his return before eating it. Then he left. He watched each child through a two way mirror during the time he was away. Some children ate the marshmallow and some waited and earned the second marshmallow. Those who ate it tended to eat it very soon after he left. Those who earned the second marshmallow used multiple strategies to keep themselves from eating the marshmallow. Some stared at the marshmallow. Some looked away from the marshmallow. Some talked to the marshmallow. Some even sang to the marshmallow. The point is some of these children delayed gratification to achieve a greater reward.

Mischel came back to these children again twelve years later. Now they were sixteen years old. They were in high school. He looked at how they were doing both academically and socially. He found that those children who at age four had delayed gratification and earned the second marshmallow were doing better academically when grades were compared. Additionally they were more socially competent, they were more self-assertive, they were better able to cope with frustration, they embraced challenges more and pursued them more energetically rather than giving up, they were more self-reliant, more trustworthy, and more dependable.

Mischel returned to these children again two years later. Now they were eighteen and taking SAT tests for college admission. In all SAT areas combined those children who had earned the second marshmallow scored an average of 210 points higher on their SAT tests. In fact, earning that extra marshmallow at age four was a far better predictor of higher SAT scores than was the child's I.Q. score.

The ability to delay gratification is critical in motivation and achievement. A child who is learning to play the piano must be able to sit and do the practicing before going out to play. If he cannot do that, he will never really learn to play the piano. When we talk about self-discipline we are talking about this delay gratification. This is an essential tool in achieving significant in our lives. When we cannot do this our life will bc filled with continual situations of giving up, of walking away, of not succeeding, and that sense of failure, of lack of control ultimately becomes very stress provoking.

The fourth domain of emotional intelligence is the ability to recognize emotions in others. Recognizing the emotions of others is the basis of empathy. This is the ultimate people skill. If we cannot recognize what another person is feeling, then we cannot possibly feel empathy for them. If we cannot feel empathy for the ups and downs, the highs and lows of another person, then we cannot connect with them. We cannot respond to them appropriately, we cannot meet their needs, we cannot comfort them.

We can see an extension of empathy, or lack of empathy, when we deal with difficult people. Difficult people tend to not be able to recognize how they are coming across. They cannot see how others are seeing them. If they could see how others were seeing them, many times they would change their behavior. The reason they cannot recognize how they are themselves being seen is that they cannot recognize the emotions of others. If I cannot recognize what you are feeling, then I cannot feel empathy for you, but I also cannot recognize what you are feeling about me, hence I do not see how I am coming across. This is typical of difficult people, this is typical of bullies, and this brings a great deal of stress into relationships.

Conversely, think about the people you really enjoy being around. These people are not merely focused on themselves... they also focus on you. They genuinely want to know how you are doing, what you have been up to, what interests you have. They demonstrate empathy and compassion. That is why we feel comfortable with and around these people.

The fifth domain of emotional intelligence is that of managing relationships. This means the ability to both establish and maintain relationships over an extended period. We all know people who get into relationships quickly but cannot stay in a relationship long term. This is because they cannot manage relationships, they cannot manage the emotions of others. This means recognizing the emotions of others, feeling empathy for them, and responding to what they are feeling in an appropriate, caring manner. This is the basis for sharing. This is the basis for really listening to others as opposed to merely waiting our turn to talk. This is the basis for taking turns. When we converse with someone who has developed this domain the conversation will not be only about them...they will be interested in us and what is going on with our lives. Someone who talks only about themselves more than likely has not developed this fifth domain of emotional intelligence.

When we look at these five domains of emotional intelligence it becomes clear that they build on each other. We cannot feel empathy for others unless we can recognize their emotions, and we cannot recognize their emotions unless we can recognize emotions in ourselves. We cannot manage relationships with others and let them have a turn unless we can manage our own emotions and delay our own gratification. We must be able to recognize our own emotions as we experience them, manage our own emotions, delay gratification, recognize emotions in others, and manage relationships with others to have a solid basis for emotional intelligence. It is never too late to develop these attributes, these skills, and we can teach them to children. Unfortunately in our society we typically do not make the effort to teach these skills to children. We model them and hope our children will learn, but we do not take the steps to teach these skills. We could, and we should. Not having these skills, these domains of emotional intelligence, results in both generating higher levels of stress in our lives and not being able to manage that stress effectively.

In Summation

1. All stress is not equal. High stress can be debilitating, while mild stress can be motivating.

2. Stress reduction is not necessarily about removing stress completely, but rather about lowering stress from a level of fight or flight to a level where it is both motivational and can be managed.

3. The level of stress we face is influenced by our own level of emotional intelligence.

4. The five domains of emotional intelligence include; the recognition of our own emotions, management of our emotions, motivating ourselves, recognizing emotions in others and feeling empathy for others, and establishing and maintaining relationships with others.

5. Having the language of emotional intelligence is a critical part of recognizing and managing emotions. It is difficult to conceptualize anything, including emotions, without having the appropriate language for it.

6. The ability to delay gratification, to stifle impulses, is crucial in motivation and achievement.

7. Difficult people often lack the capability of seeing how they come across to others, which is really an extension of the ability or lack of ability to feel empathy for others.

8. Emotional intelligence is not innate, it is learned. It is often modeled, but we typically make very little effort to teach it. It can be taught.

CHAPTER 3

Conditions that Cause Stress

You can never change the past, but unfortunately you can ruin the present by worrying too much about the future. There are things we can control in life, and there are things we cannot control in life. One of the most costly mistakes we make is that too often we focus on the things we cannot control and ignore the things that we can control. We spend our days worrying about those issues that we can do nothing about, and neglect addressing the issues we could actually impact.

So when we talk about stress and levels of stress, we must ask, what are the conditions that cause stress? Sonjia Lupine, in her research at McGill University, cites four conditions that cause stress. These are novelty, unpredictability, lack of control, and threat to ego. Every stress that we face, every stress that our loved ones face, every stress that our employees or our supervisors face fall under one or more of these four conditions.

The first condition that causes stress is novelty. Novelty means new situations. Change is an example of novelty because every change we endure means we are facing something new. Changing schools for a child is stressful because the new school is a change from the old. This is true whether the change is from moving to a new city or a new neighborhood, or merely moving from elementary school into middle school or middle school into high school. Changing jobs is stressful because it is new, it is novel.

One of my favorite little books is by Dr. Spencer Johnson, called *Who Moved My Cheese.* It is the story of four characters, two mice and two human like characters, who live in a maze. Every day they go to the Cheese station to get their cheese, but one day the cheese is gone. The story is about how these four characters deal with the change and the stress of having no cheese and finding new cheese. One of my favorite lines in the book is a question, "What would I do if I weren't afraid?"

That is a very significant question. How would we behave in a given situation if we were not afraid of the outcome? The fear and the stress that comes from change, from novelty, impacts how we act, how we perform. That question can be used in a constructive way. In the game of golf, for example, I have learned to ask myself, "How would I hit this shot if I weren't afraid of hitting the ball in the water?"

Change/novelty can have an extremely negative impact on our behavior. Have you ever worked with someone who resists change? They dig in their heels and refuse to change regardless of the consequences or of others pleading with them to do so. This is because the change is often stressful and fear producing. Even change that we willingly accept causes a certain amount of stress. Getting married is something most people go into willingly, but it does produce stress. Novelty can be a huge stressor.

A second cause of stress is that of unpredictability. This means not knowing what to expect. Novelty and unpredictability often go together, but they can come separately. You can know what to expect but still be stressed because of novelty, or you can be in a situation that is not novel but is unpredictable. Unpredictability is such a huge stressor that it is a staple of horror films. The hero is about to open the door, but what is on the other side of the door? It is unpredictable and therefore stress provoking. Or he is about to jump into the water, but what is just under the surface of the water? Or the corn stalks are moving in the corn field. What is in the cornfield? At that point in the movie the music begins to pick up in intensity because we know something is about to happen. The unpredictability creates stress.

In the more recent monster movies notice how long into the movie it is before we really get a good glimpse of the monster. We might see its eye, or its tail, but we don't see the entire creature for some time because, again, the unpredictability of what it really looks like creates stress. Movie makers have become adept at using the unpredictability factor because of just that, unpredictability is a huge stressor.

A third stressor is that of lack of control. This is when something happens, or is about to happen, or we expect it to happen and we cannot control it, or we are afraid we cannot control it. Not having control is a huge, huge stressor. This has also become a staple of horror movies. In fact, some of the most horrifying movies ever made utilize this lack of control factor. These include movies where the demon, or the being, or the creature, or the virus, or whatever actually enters the person's body and takes over. This is truly lack of control, as in movies like "The Exorcist." The lack of control factor is also used when they put heroes or heroines in situations where they have no control. For example, they put the heroine in a coffin in the ground. There is nothing she can do to save herself. If she is going to be saved someone else must do it. This is stress provoking. Often, in movies they will use unpredictability and lack of control together. The heroine is chained to the wall (lack of control) and she hears something coming down the hallway toward her (unpredictability). Is it her boyfriend coming to save her, or is it the monster? Besides horror movies, the lack of control factor is a constant in adventure films. In the James Bond movies, for example, James Bond is constantly put in situations where he has no control, where he is sure to die, yet he finds a way out. These situations are aimed at producing stress in the viewer.

In real life we often encounter situations where control or lack of control is a factor. Do you know anyone who you would term a "control freak?" What is that all about? In fact, it is really all about stress. It is about managing stress or avoiding stress. The "control freak" is attempting to control everything because when they are in control their stress is lower. When they are not in control their stress level elevates, and that is uncomfortable. This may create more stress for you dealing with this individual, but it is an attempt on their part to manage or avoid stress.

We see this factor regularly in many other situations. Claustrophobia is a good example. Claustrophobia is a fear of being in enclosed places. I would think the ultimate claustrophobic experience would be to be wedged and stuck in a small cave-like tunnel underground. We cannot move. We cannot go forward or backward. There is no room to leverage our arms to get any force behind pushing or pulling our self free. This situation would be scary for many of us, but absolutely horrifying for someone with claustrophobia. The basic issue here is the lack of control. Claustrophobia is basically a fear of lack of control.

A fear of heights or a fear of falling are other examples of this. These are basically fears of falling out of control. It is really interesting that as we live our lives we will sometimes experience times where we feel our lives are out of control. Many people, during such times, will experience a dream of falling. Our dreams are mostly visual in nature and often we dream in metaphor. A dream of falling is a visual metaphor for this sense of feeling out of control. Lack of control is a huge stressor.

The final condition that causes stress is a threat to ego. Threat to ego can refer to actual threats to our life or well-being. Examples could be situations like being in a war zone being shot at, or being threatened by a mugger on a dark street, or being confronted by a bully who is threatening us in some manner. Threat to ego also can refer to symbolic threats. These might include being overlooked or unappreciated, being disrespected or "dissed", for some it might mean being made the center of attention, it could be the threat of giving a speech. Giving a speech or talking in public is actually a huge stressor for many people. In fact it ranks high on the list of fears for a great many people. I have had acquaintances state that they would rather jump out of an airplane than have to speak in front of a crowd. I am quite sure if they were actually given that option they would not pick jumping out of an airplane, but the point they are making is that public speaking is very scary for them. Jumping out of an airplane is a real physical danger. We could die if the parachute does not open. Speaking in front of a crowd is not dangerous. We do not typically stone speakers. It is not an actual physical threat, but it is a threat to ego. We could forget what we were going to say and sound foolish, or we could say something that causes us to lose the respect or lose the esteem of others. Hence, public speaking is a huge threat to ego.

Another arena where we see a symbolic threat to ego is in sports. This is when we see athletes choke. The basketball player who is fouled and goes to the line to shoot free throws with the game on the line feels this threat and this stress. The golfer playing in the city tournament in a match play event who has to make a three foot putt to keep the match going faces this threat. Threat to ego is a major stressor in our lives.

In previous centuries this threat to ego was often more physical...our ancestors, pioneers, people coming to a new world, were often in situations where their lives were in jeopardy. In today's civilized world many of our threats are now more symbolic that actual, but they are threats non-the-less, and they do create a great deal of stress.

The Four Conditions of Stress

Novelty – Something new, a new situation, change

Unpredictability – Something that we cannot predict, we don't know what to expect

Lack of Control – Something we cannot control, or that we fear we cannot control

Threat to Ego – Something that is a threat to our life or well-being, or a symbolic threat like being insulted

Let's look at some examples of these four stressors. One issue that concerns a lot of us directly or indirectly is that of poverty. How do these four conditions of stress relate to poverty? Pretend you are a child growing up in poverty. First of all your life is filled with a great deal of novelty. One day you and your siblings are living with mom in an apartment. Then mom gets a new boyfriend and moves in with him. Now you face a different family structure. Now there is a new authority figure in the house to deal with. Now, since you live with this new boyfriend, you have moved to a different neighborhood and you have a different set of neighborhood kids to adjust to. Now you have changed schools and you have a different teacher and a different set of classmates. This is all change, it is novelty, and it generates a great deal of stress. Three months later your mom breaks up with this guy and now you move in with grandma. You now have another new home, another new family structure, another new authority figure to answer to, another new neighborhood and set of neighborhood children, another new school, another new teacher, another new set of school mates and expectations. This cycle goes on repeatedly for many children in poverty, and it provides constant stress.

Secondly, you face a great deal of unpredictability growing up in poverty. First is the unpredictability of how long will you be in this living situation, in this apartment, with this family structure, in this neighborhood, in this school, with this teacher, etc. You see the pattern of moving and you know it will happen again, so how much investment do you make and how much effort do you put into the current relationships? Also there is the unpredictability of whether mom will be home when you get home from school. If she is there will she be drunk again like she was last week? If she is drunk will she be passed out, or will she be happy and playful drunk, or will she be mean drunk? There is a significant difference. Will someone else be there with her? Will the police be there again? Will your things be out on the sidewalk because you have to move again immediately because you have been evicted or are running from the landlord? This unpredictability is a huge factor and a huge and constant stressor.

You are also facing a lack of control in your life. You cannot control when you move, where you move, who your teacher will be, when you will change schools, etc. When this scenario is repeated over and over again, you begin to feel that you have no control in your life. There have been some interesting studies done where they have asked children questions about what they think is possible in life. Children growing up in poverty typically answered those questions differently from children not in poverty. The children not in poverty tended to believe that things were possible and that they could do a variety of things in their life and with their life. The children in poverty tended to believe that things were not possible. In fact they showed more of a tendency to believe in luck, fate, and chance more than in self-determination. When you do not have control in your life it generates stress. Think about any times when you really felt things were out of control in your life. How much stress did that generate for you? This is often what children growing up in poverty experience.

Finally, as you grow up in poverty you feel a threat to ego. Some of this is a real physical threat because you live in neighborhoods where you may have to fight for survival, and some of it is symbolic threat. For example, children in poverty do not do as well in school. This is often not because they do not have the capability. Rather it is because they have moved around a great deal. Consequently they have missed things educationally because of moving from classroom to classroom from school to school. They have had to focus their attention more on survival than on getting their homework done. Also they have typically not been asked the same kind of questions at home. They are not asked questions like, "What did you do in school today? Did you get your homework done? Do you understand that?" That kind of reinforcement that school is really important often does not exist. The result is, they do not do as well in school, they do not make as good grades, and they interpret that as, "I'm not as smart, I'm not as capable, I'm slow, and I'm dumb." This is a significant threat to ego. If you really feel you cannot compete and if you believe it is all fate, luck, and chance anyway, then why try. It becomes very easy to give up.

This is not a book about poverty, but my point is that growing up in poverty creates high levels of stress. Earlier I mentioned that when we experience high stress we are in fight or flight or prepared to go into fight or flight. When we are constantly in fight or flight mode we are ready to fight or flee from situations. If this is constant, we actually learn patterns of flight or running away from issues. This is what often happens in poverty. Children learn to run from stress rather than face it and resolve it. A common factor we see in poverty is that of single parent families. Why is this so common? When individuals have grown up in poverty and learned patterns of running from issue rather than facing them, and then when an issue or problem comes up in the relationship, the first choice to flee, to run away. So, in this case, one of the partners in the relationship runs off. Is this really so surprising in light of how they have learned to deal with stress? If we really want to change this in our society we need to address the stress factor of growing up in poverty, and what this teaches children.

Another example of stress would be when we get a promotion at work. Getting a promotion creates stress because of the novelty of the situation. We are performing different acts. The promotion may require supervising others, which is an added responsibility over and above just worrying about our self. Now we must keep up with what others are doing and make sure they are doing a good job.

Not only is a promotion novel, but it also creates unpredictability. Getting a promotion may involve multiple new demands beyond merely supervision others, and there will be things that crop up that no one told us about. These kinds of issues always seem to come up at the worst times. We are trying to figure out the basics and suddenly we are dealing with an entirely different issue that we had not expected. This is stressful.

There is also an element of lack of control in a promotion. We can no longer just do our job, now we must deal with all the problems of the people we are supervising. We may think we have an agenda for the day dealing with issues "a, b, and c", and suddenly that agenda goes out the window because we have to deal with issues "x, y, and z" that our staff brought to us. Then our boss comes into the office in the afternoon and wants to see what we have accomplished with "a, b, and c". He also informs us that we will have to make a trip out of town to have a face to face meeting with some clients or some suppliers. This lack of control over how our time is spent creates stress.

Finally there is the stress from threat to ego. When we get that promotion we may feel very proud, but then we are faced with tasks we are not sure we know how to handle and the uncertainty of whether we can actually do the job correctly creeps into our mind. What if we are demoted or fired because we don't measure up to their expectations? We sense our new staff is also watching us wondering if we can be an effective leader. This creates stress.

The bottom line is that these four conditions, novelty, unpredictability, lack of control, and threat to ego are the conditions that generate stress in our lives. Think about the individual stressors in your life. Are they from novelty, unpredictability, lack of control, or threat to ego? All of our stresses fall under one or more of these conditions. If we understand that, then the next step in managing stress in any situation is to address the specific condition or conditions that are causing us stress. In the second part of this book we will discuss addressing these specific conditions.

In Summation

1. The four conditions that cause stress are novelty, unpredictability, lack of control, and threat to ego.

2. Change is an example of novelty. Some people resist change at all cost because of the stress that it brings.

3. Unpredictability occurs when we do not know what to expect. The producers of horror movies use unpredictability as a staple because of the stress it generates.

4. A feeling of lack of control occurs when things are beyond our control or we perceive that we cannot control them. "Control freaks" are all about trying to control everything because it lowers their stress. Claustrophobia and a fear of heights are examples of lack of control issues.

5. Threat to ego can be from a real physical threat, as when we are in a truly dangerous situation, or it can come from a symbolic threat, as when we feel disrespected or put down.

6. The four conditions that generate stress can be seen when we look at such issues as poverty or issues concerning employment, but these are merely examples.

CHAPTER 4

How the Brain Works when Stressed

Success is subjective. If you asked Donald Trump to define success you would certainly get a different answer than if you asked the same question of Mother Teresa. If you attempted something about six hundred times and were successful on fifteen occasions, is that success? Some might say no, but this is exactly what Fred Couples has done. From the beginning of his career until he turned fifty he played in nearly six hundred golf tournaments, and he won fifteen times. He will be going into the PGA Hall of Fame someday. Was he successful? Success is subjective, but so is failure. Neither success nor failure is truly an external event, but rather they are internal attitudes. How often do we create stress in our lives by the internal attitudes we hold?

Another way of looking at and understanding stress is through understanding a little about brain functioning. Dr. Elkhonon Goldberg, in his book *The Executive Brain*, talks about the locus of control of brain functioning. He states that we used to think that the locus of control for different functions was set in different hemispheres of the brain. For example, we thought that language ability was a left hemisphere function and that musical ability was a right hemisphere function.

When we examined adults who had strokes, this notion seemed correct. An adult who had a stroke in the left hemisphere of his brain certainly had more language issues to overcome than someone who had a stroke in the right hemisphere. However, a few years ago we began noticing stokes in children. Not as many children have strokes as adults, but when they do what became apparent was that it was a stroke in the right hemisphere of the brain, not the left hemisphere, which caused language issues. But if language is a left hemisphere function, as we thought, how could this be? Well, it became obvious that some more research needed to be done...that we did not understand the issues around left hemisphere/right hemisphere as well as we thought we did.

What has since been learned is that the loci of control for different functions, such as language, can and do shift. The way the brain actually functions is that novelty (that is processing novel functions and ideas) is a right hemisphere function, and processing routine is a left hemisphere function. This is how the brain breaks down tasks.

This makes sense when we look at language. For an adult, language is a routine function. The way we speak, the way we use language is routine and hence is processed in the left hemisphere. We may learn new words or idioms from time to time, but the way we use language is routine. Language is routine unless we begin to learn a foreign language. If we begin learning Spanish, for example, our use of Spanish will be processed in the right hemisphere until such time as we begin to be fluent in Spanish. If and when that happens, the locus of control for speaking Spanish will shift to the left hemisphere.

For a child, on the other hand, language is novel and hence processed in the right hemisphere. Young children have no language. Then they begin learning a word here and there, "Mama" or "Dada." Then they begin to put a few words together, "Me drink." Eventually they are speaking in longer and longer sentences, and eventually their use of language becomes routine. When that occurs, their brain will shift the locus of control for language from the right hemisphere to the left hemisphere.

Musical ability works the same way. We used to think that musical ability was a right hemisphere function. The reason we thought that was because the people studied were not musicians. Musical ability is a right hemisphere function for most of us because we don't read or play music, hence figuring out the notes on a page and hitting the corresponding key on a piano is a new or novel, right hemisphere function. For a musician, however, it is a routine function. A pianist looks at the notes on a sheet of music and reads them like you or I would read a book, and this process is occurring in their left hemisphere.

The same is true for all functions. If I play chess it is a right hemisphere function...I'm definitely thinking my way through it. For a chess master, when the brain is hooked up to see what part is really working, it is the left hemisphere that is predominately engaged because for the chess master this is a routine function. Whatever behaviors we perform habitually will ultimately become routine for us. This means that for some people playing golf becomes routine and hence a left hemisphere function. For others it may be tennis, or bowling, or typing. For whatever we do that becomes routine, know that the locus of control for that behavior has shifted to the left hemisphere.

> New thoughts, new behaviors, novelty are a right hemisphere functions. Routine actions, routine behaviors, habits become left hemisphere functions.

New thoughts, new behaviors, novelty are right hemisphere functions. Routine actions, routine behaviors, habits become left hemisphere functions. Now remember what we discussed in Chapter 1. When we go into fight or flight mode the locus of control shifts to the limbic system. The limbic system is referred to as a system because it includes the amygdala, the hippocampus, the thalamus, etc. However, the limbic system is also a place because the structures that make up this system are located in the deeper part of the brain, under the cerebrum. The limbic system is often called the emotional part of the brain. It is really a little more complex than that, but basically the limbic system takes over in times of threat to become more highly attuned to danger. If you talk to someone who is in a state of fight or flight it can be difficult to get their attention. They may have trouble listening to your words, focusing on what you are saying because they are looking for danger cues. In fact, we know that the language centers in the brain get less oxygen when we are in fight or flight. The limbic system takes over at this point to focus on whatever threat is out there, and the locus of control shifts to the limbic system for survival. This is why, for example, when we get nervous talking in front of a group of people we can forget what we were trying to say. What has happened is that the locus of control has shifted from the right or left cerebral hemisphere to the limbic system.

So, let's recap. When we are doing something novel the locus of control is in the right hemisphere. When we are doing routine tasks the locus of control is in the left hemisphere. When we are under stress, frightened, or in a highly emotional state the locus of control is in the limbic system. The locus of control for brain functioning can and does shift regularly between these brain areas. It does this all the time. Knowing this, however, means that we can learn to shift it at will, when we want.

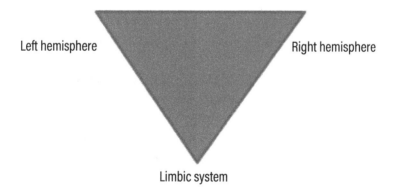

Left hemisphere   Right hemisphere

Limbic system

(For the mere sake of visualization I like to think of it as the triangle pictured above, the locus of control can shift between these areas.)

Let me give some examples. Looking at sports is a good place to begin because it is easier to see. In fact, some of the best examples of this entire process are evident in the game of golf. In amateur golf tournaments when golfers are playing a match play event, which means they are competing against one other person at a time, it is easy to watch the result of stress on the play. The result is typically referred to as "choking." One or both payers can play at a certain level, but suddenly when the match is on the line one or both players will begin hitting bad shots, missing short putts, taking their eyes off the ball, etc.

I remember one occasion when I was attempting to qualify for a city golf tournament. We were qualifying in foursomes, and the individual who's score card I was keeping (you don't keep your own) was a young man who had played on his high school golf team. He was a good golfer, but he was obviously nervous. This was the first time he had attempted to qualify for the city tournament's championship flight. His nerves got the better of him and he hit a few poor shots. Those poor shots led to more poor shots and he was out of the running for making the championship flight quite early. While he was capable of shooting scores in the low 70's, and sometimes even in the 60's, on this day he shot over 100. He was so frustrated he did not return for the second day of qualifying. The point is, he did not forget how to play golf, but rather his stress level got so high he could not focus on golf. His limbic system was in control when the control should have been in his left hemisphere.

This is easy to see in amateur golf tournaments, but we sometimes see it in professional events. How many times have we seen scenarios where a young professional golfer who has never won an event will suddenly find himself in the lead? Then, when he notices the score board and realizes he is leading, he will promptly bogey or double bogey the next hole? This has to do with stress and the locus of control. We don't see this happen as often in professional golf as we do in amateur golf, but we do see it. One of the reasons it is not as readily apparent in professional golf is not only that the skill level is higher, but more because professional golfers have been taught to use routine. They have learned the importance of the strict, pre-shot routine.

Sports psychologists tell us to develop such pre-shot routines for golf. This might include such things as taking a few deep breaths, taking a specific number of practice swings, visualizing the shot and the ball flight, stepping up to the ball exactly the same way, having the same swing thoughts, and then striking the ball. When we do this we will typically strike the ball better and get a better result from our efforts.

Examine what is really happening here. We are becoming stressed because we need to hit a good shot to get the ball over a lake or to keep it from going into a wooded area. As the stress level rises, as when more is at stake, then the locus of control will actually shift to the limbic system and the result is that we actually perform worse. By going through the pre-shot routines what we are doing is attempting to move the locus of control back to the left hemisphere, because we do actually know how to hit the golf shot. The routines calm us. The routines allow us to do what we have learned to do. At that point in the competition we do not want the locus of control to be in the limbic system, we do not want emotions taking over. We also do not want the locus of control in the right hemisphere, we don't want to be thinking our way through the golf swing because that is a sure recipe for disaster. What we want is to get the brain out of the way and let our routines, the routines we have learned about hitting a golf ball, take over. That is by far the best chance we have of being successful and striking the ball properly.

The same is true of basketball. Basketball is a fast paced game that goes up and down the court. Then someone is fouled and everything stops. One player goes to the free throw line, the rest of his team is watching, the other team is watching, the coaches are watching, the fans are watching, and he is expected to put the ball in the basket. This is an opportune time to choke. Even players who are considered good shots will miss free throws at critical times in a game. Again, this is because during the flow of the game they are reacting. Emotions don't have as much time to take over. But when everything is stopped and they realize just how important this shot is, they choke.

What about those players who don't choke? What do consistently good free throw shooters have in common? They all have a routine they go through before the free throw shot. It does not matter what the routine is, but just that there is a routine. Years ago I remember watching Steve Alford at the free throw line. He played for Indiana University and was an amazing free throw shooter, even in clutch situations. Before every free throw he touched his socks and then his shorts. He probably did something routine with the ball in his hands also, but the point is he went through his routines.

Such routines are not merely superstition. It may be a superstition for a player, but the real importance of the matter is that by utilizing a routine of some kind they are shifting the locus of control back to the left hemisphere. If I were a basketball coach, one aspect of the game I would definitely address would be to make sure all of my players had a set routine they went through before each and every free throw. Hitting free throws in practice is not the same thing as hitting them when the game is on the line and stress is creeping into the equation. Having a pre-shot routine, that is used during practice and then in the game, will improve free throw shooting.

With baseball we can see the same thing. How many players have a ritual or a routine they go through before getting into the batter's box? Some will loosen and tighten their hitting gloves. Some will kiss an icon of some kind they wear on a chain around their neck. Some will make a religious sign. A number of ball players undoubtedly have mental routines they also go through, but the point is they go through routines. Again, it may be superstition on the part of some ball players, but the significant thing is they hit better when they go through these rituals. It is not the superstition that is making them perform better, it is that they are shifting the locus of control back to the left hemisphere thus allowing their body to do what they have taught it to do.

My favorite sports example comes from platform diving. During the 2000 Olympics Laura Wilkinson, a diver on the United States Olympic team, won the gold medal. In the 2004 Olympics she was back on the team and back in the gold medal round. During an interview she was asked how she dove. Her reply was that she dove "brain dead." The interviewer asked what she meant by "brain dead." Laura stated that she had practiced these dives hundreds and hundreds of times. She knew the dives and she knew what to do to perform each dive well. However, she stated that if she began to get stressed, which is when the locus of control is switching to the limbic system, she doesn't dive as well. She also said that if she tries to think her way through a dive, which means the locus of control is in the right hemisphere, she messes up. What she tries to do is simply go through her routines, attempting to get the locus of control back to the left hemisphere, and let her body do what she has taught it to do. Laura did not use the terms right hemisphere, left hemisphere, or limbic system, but that is exactly what she was doing and exactly what she was actually talking about.

Let's move on to some non-sports examples of this locus of control issue. Grief and trauma provide an excellent example. Cheri Lovre, who is a well-known crisis intervention specialist, tells a story of a woman who was suffering from trauma. To re-cap this story, the woman had a teenage daughter who was shot and killed by a gunman. Her thoughts were constantly centered on the fact that her daughter's life was ended prematurely, that her daughter would not graduate from high school, that her daughter would never get to go to the prom, that her daughter would not go to college as she had planned, etc. She could not get past these kinds of thoughts. She could not heal.

Eventually this woman tried seeing a therapist. The therapist kept asking her what she felt about her daughter's death. Her thoughts and feelings were varied, and confusing, and difficult to put into language. She quickly stopped attending these counseling sessions. The woman was also having nightmares on a regular basis. Her recurring nightmare was seeing her daughter standing before her, seeing the gunman standing before her, watching the gunman as he aimed his gun at her daughter, watching the gunman begin to pull the trigger, and at that moment she would awaken in a heart pounding panic. This woman was stuck in trauma. She could not get past this event. She could not grieve her daughter's death, move past it, or heal from it.

Then someone asked her to tell the story of her daughter's life. To put her life into words...to put her daughter's life into language. Now she was not being asked to talk about her feelings about her daughter's death, but rather to tell the story of her daughter's life. This she could do. She told about her daughter's birth, learning to walk, learning to talk, her pre-school years, her early school years, pictures she brought home from school that they hung on the refrigerator, friends she made, skills she learned, interests she developed, boys she liked, plans she made for her future. The story of her life included the shooting and her death, but that was only a part of the story.

Look at what was happening. Language, for adults, is a routine function. It is a left hemisphere function. Being stuck in trauma, in the negative emotions of that shooting, meant that the locus of control of her thought patterns was stuck in the limbic system, the emotional center of the brain. By telling the story of her daughter's life, which took a long time, she was putting it into language, she was moving the thoughts to the left hemisphere. The effect of this was to begin to move her out of trauma. In fact, this woman stated that the evening of the day she told the story of her daughter's life, she again had the dream. This time, however, it did not end with the gunman pulling the trigger and her awakening in terror. This time the gunman pulled the trigger, shot her daughter, and her daughter fell to the ground and died. But this time she went to her daughter's side, took her daughter's hand, and told her daughter how much she loved her and missed her. She was finally beginning the process of grieving. Now she could think about her daughter and not merely focus on the shooting. Now she could remember the good times and the bad times, the friends and the parties, the accomplishments and the disappointments. By shifting the locus on control to the left hemisphere through telling the story of her daughter's life, she was able to begin to grieve.

We used this same strategy when we had a death at school. I worked as Director of the Social Services Department in a public school for a number of years, and over those years there were occasions when we had students and/or faculty die. On one occasion after school, near the very end of a school year, an eighth grade student died in a skate boarding accident. He was a very likeable young man and a very popular student. We knew that the following day, as word spread through the school about his death, we would have lots of students experiencing trauma. That next day we had a contingency of professional staff there as his death was announced in classrooms. We were waiting to talk with students, either individually or in small groups , who needed to talk.

One of the key strategies was not to ask other students how they felt about his death. They may have felt lots of things. The feelings were multiple and difficult to understand, and hence often difficult to put into words. Asking how they feel will more often lead to students clamming up. They will either say they don't want to talk, or they are so confused they cannot put things into words. Instead, the strategy was to ask them to tell stories about the young man who died. How did you meet him, what's the funniest thing you remember about him, what was it about him you most liked, what stories do you remember about him, etc.? They can tell these stories, they can put that into words, into language. This means they are engaging the left hemisphere. This allows them to move out of or past the trauma and move into grief. Getting them to begin the grieving process is important. Grieving is a functional necessity. Grieving allows us to heal from the trauma. If we do not grieve, if we stuff these kinds of emotions, then the next loss we suffer will bring back all of these feelings in addition to the current ones. This is when we get overwhelmed. Hence, the goal is to help students move into grief to begin to heal, and we do that by getting them to put things into stories...into language.

The same is true if we have ever had a friend or relative who lost someone close, and we go to the funeral home for the viewing. How do they respond if we ask them how they are or how they are doing? Typically they will state that they are fine or they will be okay. Those questions do not get them to open up. They may not know how they are. They may not be able to put it into words. They may be feeling a wide range of emotions that are confusing and even scary for them. So if we really want to help them, what do we ask? We ask them to tell the stories of the deceased. How they met, how they proposed, where they went on their honeymoon, what are their favorite memories of the deceased, what are their funniest memories, etc.? If there are pictures, ask them about the pictures. Where was this taken, what were you doing there, etc.? Get them to tell the stories because this gets them to put things into language, and since language is a routine function, a left hemisphere function for adults, it helps them begin to grieve.

Another example can be seen in working with children with autism. If you have ever worked with a child with autism you know that when their routine is disrupted they can become very agitated. Some might cry or scream, some might throw a fit or even become violent, and some might even run away. If you have ever had to chase after a child with autism who has taken off, you begin to understand this. Does this sound like fight or flight? That is exactly what it is. They are going into fight or flight because their routine was disrupted. The routines they have, the rituals they must perform, calm them in this scary world they are living in. When these routines are disrupted it is scary, it is stressful for them. The best way to help a child with autism calm down is to get them back into their routines as quickly as possible. That means we must know what their routines are. So to help them calm down we begin to talk about their routines and get them back into a routine atmosphere doing a routine function as quickly as possible. What we are attempting to do is to help them shift back into the left hemisphere, because the traumatic disruption to their routines shifted their brain functioning, their locus of control, to the limbic system.

Understanding how the locus of control shifts in different situations, and what we sometimes can and do to shift it without even realizing what we are actually doing is important. With this information, it means that we can learn to shift the locus of control at will. When we are becoming stressed we can do something to utilize routine and reduce the stress and the impact that stress might have on our thinking and our performance. In the second part of this book we will discuss these possibilities further.

In Summation

1. The locus of control shifts easily and frequently between the left hemisphere, the right hemisphere, and the limbic system.

2. When we are doing something novel, something we have to think about, the locus of control is predominantly in the right hemisphere.

3. When we are doing something that is routine for us the locus of control is predominantly in the left hemisphere.

4. When strong emotions are involved the locus of control shifts predominantly to the limbic system.

5. Language is an example of something that is a left hemisphere function for adults because it is routine, but a right hemisphere function for children because language is still being learned and is still a novel process.

6. By utilizing this knowledge, we can use routine to shift the locus of control to calm ourselves in sports, we can use it to move from trauma to grief, and we can use it whenever we face situations that are stressful.

CHAPTER 5

Stress and Mindset

The very basics of quantum physics are about attraction. Ions have positive and negative charges, they attract and they repel other ions. This is the very core of energy, the very core of matter... magnetism...attraction and repulsion. Attraction and repulsion are also the basics of human relationships. We attract others or we repel others. This may be conscious or unconscious, but we either bring people into our lives or we keep them out or even push them away based on our own positive or negative charges. These positive or negative charges are created by our thoughts, by the way we think. It is created and maintained by the habitual thought patterns we keep. Consistent negative thinking drives others away, it repels them. Likewise, people who are consistently positive are easy to be around, we are drawn to them, we are attracted to them. When we are not happy with life we can change our lives, we can change our relationships by creating a more positive charge with our thoughts. The habitual thoughts we keep, that we allow ourselves to have, are the most powerful forces in our lives.

Making assumptions is a common part of everyday functioning. We all do it, and we do it all of the time. When we meet someone new they make a first impression on us; the way they look, the way they talk, the way they act, their mannerisms, their dialect, the way they put sentences together, etc. We take that in, and based on that we make assumptions about that person. We tend to make more positive assumptions about those people who seem most like ourselves, but never-the-less we are making assumptions about them. They are doing the same about us. Some of these assumptions prove right, but sometimes they prove wrong.

We cannot help but do this. We have been trained to do it. When we are very young we have toys and blocks that we learn to sort by height, by shape, by size, and by color. Putting things in categories is how we learn to think, to organize, to learn sameness and differences, to discriminate between seemingly similar objects or ideas. When we use it against people as in sexual discrimination or racial discrimination, then it becomes problematic in society, but the way the brain works is a matter of helping us make critical decisions. This is the basis of assumptions.

We also make assumptions about activities. There is a certain etiquette to riding in an elevator. We get on and turn around to face the front, not the back or the sides. We don't stand too close to the other people on the elevator unless it is crowded and we have no choice. We don't sing on the elevator. If another person is on the elevator we stand over to the side rather than right in front of them or right behind them. When someone does any of these things they violate our assumptions about proper elevator etiquette and we get away from that individual as quickly as we can.

The point is, we make assumptions all the time. We are not even aware we are making assumptions a great deal of the time, but these assumptions impact our thoughts and our behaviors whether we realize we have them or not. And to take it one step further, and possibly most importantly, we make assumptions about ourselves. The assumptions we make about ourselves significantly impact who we are and how we function.

The mindset we have is a large part of the assumptions we make about ourselves. Carol Dweck of Stanford University wrote a book called *Mindset*. She discusses mindset as the way we see ourselves, the way we see our abilities. In other words, the assumptions we are making about ourselves. Some people think, for example, that their intelligence is fixed. They believe that their mental abilities are set, that they do not change. Other people believe that their intelligence, their mental abilities, can grow, can change, can be expanded by what we do and the efforts we make. We all believe one way or the other. We would call one way of thinking a fixed mindset, and the other a growth mindset. What do you believe? Think about that for a moment. Do you believe that your intelligence is set, that your mental abilities are set, or do you believe that you can influence your intelligence and your mental abilities with effort? Whether we believe in a fixed mindset or a growth mindset profoundly affects the way we lead our lives.

There was an interesting study described by Dweck with junior high students. Seventh grade students were asked if they believed that intelligence was a fixed trait or whether it was something that could be altered, developed, or enhanced. Based on the answers each student gave, they were put on one of two lists...a fixed mindset list or a growth mindset list. Then, knowing that mathematics becomes much harder and more complicated in junior high, they watched the math scores of these two groups over the next several years. Comparing the two groups as a whole, the math scores of the group with the growth mindset improved over the next two years, while the math scores of the group with the fixed mindset declined.

The difference here is what we believe. If we believe we cannot do something then it becomes easy to give up, to stop trying, to not put forth the effort. If, on the other hand, we believe that if we work harder we can get it, we can learn it, we can do it, then it becomes a matter of just putting forth the effort. Mindset was crucial with these students.

Since the mindset students had seemed so important in learning math, the researchers went back to incoming groups of seventh grade students to see if they could teach students to have a growth mindset. They went to groups of students who already were having trouble with math, who were already at the bottom. They took these students and divided them into two equal groups based on how they were doing in math. One group was taught study skills, as would typically be done with struggling students. The other group was given a mini course in how the brain works. They were taught that the brain changes as we learn, which it does. They were taught that as we learn something and go over it again and again so that it becomes more and more familiar, neuro-pathways are forged, the dendrites become bushier, brain activity in those specific areas increases, and the speed of these connections increases. This slowly and gradually alters our ability to think about these concepts. In other words it raises our intelligence level. It won't jump Intelligence by thirty points, but it does elevate it over time. We can especially see this intelligence increase with young children when we engage them in brain enhancing activities like music.

There was an interesting study done by E. Glenn Schallenberg of the University of Toronto. He wanted to show that teaching music could raise I.Q. scores. He measured the intelligence quotient for a number of kindergarten students. Then he divided them into four equal groups based on their I.Q. scores. The first group was taught music through giving them piano lessons. The second group was taught music by teaching them to sing. The third group was not taught music, but rather was given drama or acting lessons. The fourth group was the control group and was given no special lessons. At the end of the year he again measured their I.Q. levels. What he found was that the first group, the one given piano lessons, improved their I.Q scores by about seven points per student. The group that was taught to sing raised their I.Q. scores by roughly six points per child. The group that was given acting lessons improved their I.Q. scores by five points per child. The group that was the control group raised their I.Q. scores by about four points per child. This study showed several things. First, that the enrichment of kindergarten is important, because the group that had only kindergarten elevated their I.Q. scores by four points per child. Schallenberg also demonstrated that teaching music, specifically keyboarding, can elevate a child's I.Q. scores within a short period of time. They scored three points higher than the control group. The point is that Intelligence, or what we refer to commonly as one's I.Q., is not as stable or set as we once thought. It can be elevated through various activities that cause the brain to forge neural pathways. This also means, however, that by doing nothing with our minds, by being a couch potato, by refusing to engage in mental gymnastics, we may have a negative impact on our own I.Q. level.

An interesting aside to Schallenberg's study came with the group of young actors. This group demonstrated an increase in social skills that was not evident in any of the other groups. Acting basically is learning to recognize and portray emotions. To portray or act out emotions we must first be able to recognize them. This is the first domain of emotional intelligence. This group, having learned to recognize emotions, also began to demonstrate empathy for their fellow students. They could recognize what others were feeling, feel empathy, and respond to that empathy appropriately by allowing others to take a turn, by sharing, etc. Although this outcome was not one that was envisioned as an outcome of this study, it was significant enough that Scallenberg felt he must report it.

Now back to these 7th grade students. After teaching one group study skills and giving the other group a course in how the brain works, they again watched the math scores of both groups over the next two years. What they found was that the group who had been taught how the brain works surpassed the other group significantly in their math abilities. By teaching them a different mindset they improved their math scores.

Here is what happens with mindset, according to Dweck. The fixed mindset creates an urgency to prove itself. If we believe that our abilities are set, that our intelligence is set, then we are always on trial. We are always being judged. We must keep proving our worth, that we are capable, that we are smart. If we feel we cannot prove our worth, then we stop trying. We give up. Every task is about succeeding or failing, not about learning and growing. Either we measure up or we don't.

The growth mindset, on the other hand, begins with the notion that where we are is the starting point not the final destination of our development. We believe we can get better at a task, at any task, if we put forth the effort. We can improve our abilities, and we can even increase our intelligence regarding the issues we pursue. While the fixed mindset is about validating itself, the growth mindset is about developing itself.

> While the fixed mindset is about validating itself,
>
> the growth mindset is about developing itself.

We have all witnessed children, teenagers, college students, or even adults who give up. We certainly see this in high school. We see students who have a fixed mindset regarding their abilities. They believe they cannot learn to read well, or do math well, etc. So what happens is they give up and they drop out. Most often they have dropped out mentally long before they are of the age where they can legally drop out of school. This is tragic because often the reason they are drop outs, the reason they are failing, is not because of their abilities but rather because of their mindset about their abilities.

We see the same thing at the college level. How many students had a fairly easy time in high school, but when they entered college they found the competition was tougher? Those with a fixed mindset are more often those who drop out during or after their freshman year and never return. They see tougher competition, they don't believe they have the abilities to compete at this higher level, and they end up giving up and going home. Again, this is not because they do not have the ability to do it, it is because their mindset is such that they believe they do not have the ability to do it.

Mindset also significantly affects effort. In the fixed mindset world effort is a bad thing. If we were truly smart we would not have to work hard to get that "A." Have you ever listened to student conversations after a test? Some will say things like, "I got an 'A' and I didn't even open the book, I barely looked at my notes, I hardly studied at all, etc." These are fixed mindset comments. What they are really saying is "I'm smart, I don't have to put effort into it." Other students might say, "I got an 'A' because I really worked hard, I studied all night, I worked my tail off, etc." These are growth mindset comments. They are acknowledging that it is via work and effort that they achieved something special.

Children, adolescents, or adults...we all want to succeed. People with fixed mindsets want to succeed and people with growth mindsets want to succeed. The difference is that with a fixed mindset, if we believe we will not or cannot succeed, we don't try. We learn not to attempt tasks if it appears we might not be successful at them.

There was an interesting study done with four-year olds. These children were initially asked questions to determine whether they had a fixed mindset or a growth mindset. Yes, even by age four this mindset issue is developing. The children were then allowed to play with jigsaw puzzles. They played with these puzzles long enough that they became familiar with the puzzles and could put them together successfully each time. Then they were given an option. They were shown some different jigsaw puzzles. The new puzzles were a little harder than those they had previously worked. The children were asked whether they wanted to continue playing with the puzzles they already had, or would they like to play with the new puzzles, but they could not do both. What they found was that the children with a fixed mindset chose to continue playing with the familiar, easier puzzles. They had already proven themselves with these puzzles. They were already successful with these. They might not be successful with the newer, harder puzzles. The children with the growth mindset chose the harder puzzles. They were willing to take the risk. They did not see it as a test of their abilities, but rather as another challenge they could tackle. Even at this young age the mindset we have impacts our willingness to try new tasks, to risk new experiences, or to cling to what we know we can do and not venture into uncharted waters.

When a fixed mindset individual fails at something it measures them, it invalidates their abilities, they feel like a failure. Failure becomes transformed from an act, "I failed", to an identity, "I'm a failure." It invalidates them permanently in their own eyes. With some students this means they don't dare fail. We see some students who work so hard on every task, on every assignment, studying for every task that they are so over-prepared there is no possibility they will not get that "A." They don't dare fail because that would invalidate them in their eyes and, they believe, in the eyes of everyone else. Know anyone like that? With other students it comes out as not caring. They would rather fail because they did not try than fail because they tried and were proven not up to the task. When we look at students who are afraid to try things, or who over-achieve, we would do well to examine the mindset they have.

Mindset is also important in how we praise children. Some interesting studies have been done. In one such study adolescents were given difficult non-verbal problems to solve. After a period of time those conducting the testing began praising the students. The adolescents were divided into two groups and the praise was handed out differently in these two groups. In the first group the adolescents were told they were doing well because "they were smart." In other words they were being praised for their intellect. In the second group they were told that they were doing well because "they were working hard." These adolescents were being praised for their effort. Praising ability or intellect pushes us toward a fixed mindset. "I'm smart, that's why I'm doing well." Praising work or effort pushes us toward a growth mindset. "I'm doing well because I'm working hard."

Both of these groups performed equally well before the "praising" was started. After the praising began, however, other things began to change. In fact two things changed. The first thing that changed was their willingness to go on, to try solving more problems. The adolescents were asked if they could go on and do more, and those who had been praised for their effort readily agreed to continue. Those who had been praised for being smart, however, were more reluctant to go on. They had already proven that they were smart. The only place to go was down. If they didn't do as well on the new test items maybe those who had praised them would determine they were not as smart as they had previously looked. There was a risk in continuing for the "smart" students, which was not present for the "effort" students. If they failed now their "smartness" would be questioned.

In addition to the difference in willingness to continue, a difference in how the groups were actually performing on these problems was noted. The group praised for effort continued to perform at the same level as they had previously. The group praised for being smart was now performing worse. There was more pressure on this group because they felt a need to continue performing at a high level, so pressure and stress mounted, and when we are under stress we typically do not perform as well at any task.

I have been talking a great deal about children and adolescents because this issue of mind set is so easy to see at this level. However, mindset affects all of us. It affects where we are, how we got here, and where we are going in work, in relationships, and in life. The main issue here is the mindset we have. If we have a fixed mindset, if we believe our abilities including intellectual abilities are set, that will impact how we function. It will impact what we try, what we attempt, what we get involved in, whether we are willing to take risks and when we do attempt new things how we think we are being perceived. If we have a growth mindset, if we believe that we can do just about anything if we want it enough and are willing to put in the time and effort, then we are more willing to try new things, to take on tasks that seem daunting, to take a risk here and there.

The mindset we have impacts the stress that we feel. This means it can impact both the things that stress us or don't stress us, and the level of stress we experience in the various situations that stress us. The important thing to remember, however, is that mindset can be changed. Mindset can be altered. Just as mindset was altered with adolescents by teaching them about how the brain works, we can alter our own mindset. We can shift both what we think and how we think. What we think is learned. We can always learn something new, a new way to look at things. How we think is habit. We can certainly learn and practice new habits. Both of these are within our control. We will discuss these concepts in the second part of this book.

In Summation

1. We make assumptions daily. They are a part of our lives. We are often not even aware we are doing so.

2. We make assumptions about ourselves and the assumptions we make about ourselves significantly affect how we function.

3. Our mindset is an assumption about ourselves. We either believe that our intelligence and our abilities are set, or we believe that they can be enhanced, changed by what we do and what we don't do.

4. Having a growth mindset is a critical piece in learning, it affects learning.

5. I.Q., which we once believed was set, can actually be increased by what we do with our minds.

6. Mindset also influences what we are willing to attempt in life and whether we give up when faced with difficult tasks or keep on trying.

7. Mindset influences effort and how we look at effort. Effort can be seen as a good thing or as a bad thing depending on our mindset.

8. How we are praised and how we praise children influences effort and willingness to take on challenges, it influences mindset.

9. Mindset affects what we attempt in life, what challenges we take on, the effort we are willing to put toward a task, our willingness to take a risk and very much it influences the level of stress we face.

CHAPTER 6

Stress and Automatic Thought Patterns

We are often caught up in an "internal dialogue." Our consciousness consists of a constant internal self-dialogue. This dialogue is an endless mental conversation that wanders from the past to the future, through our hopes and our fears, encompassing our fantasies and our desires, lingering on arguments and schemes. When we do this we often miss a great deal of what is going on around us. We can miss the beautiful sunset, the birds singing in the morning, the joy of the companionship of the person beside us. When we can truly relax we can momentarily get away from this internal dialogue and experience more of the preset. This is what happens with meditation. The present is typically more peaceful for us than fretting over the past or worrying about the future. Make the effort to learn to enjoy the "now." Taking time each day to enjoy the "now," to meditate, brings inner peace.

Another issue that must be addressed is that of the habitual way we think, the habitual thoughts we have. Let's talk for just a moment about habits. I need to ask you to try something. Please set your book or kindle down and cross your arms over your chest. Now, uncross your arms and cross them the other way, with the other arm on top and the other hand tucked under your other arm. If you went along and did that, how did it feel when you tried to cross your arms a different way? For most of us, it feels strange. Why? It is because we have a habit of doing it one way. Some people have done it both ways so it feels natural either way, but for most of us we cross our arms one way. This is insignificant in our lives, which way we cross our arms, but the point is that it is a habit. We have many habits. We have more habits than we realize, and there is nothing wrong with having habits. They help us get through the day. For most of us, when we tried to cross our arms a different way we had to think our way through it. If you had to think about it every time you crossed your arms, or had to think about all the other things we do habitually every day, we wouldn't get a whole lot done. So habits can be good.

On the other hand, habits can be bad. Habits can be negative. Habits can cause us problems. Habits can elevate our stress level. Some of us get into habits such as having a snack at night when we watch television. We get that bowl of popcorn or ice cream around eight o'clock when the prime time shows come on. The issue is, we are not eating because we are hungry, we are eating because it has become a habit. The eight o'clock hour and sitting in front of the television is a cue to eat. Then we worry about losing weight. We all have some habits we wish we did not have.

We not only have behavioral habits, we have thought habits. We have habitual ways we think about things, and these thought habits can also be either good or bad. Think about road rage. What is it really? Do we suddenly, out of the blue, fly into a rage because someone cut in front of us on the highway? That is not what happens. What actually happens is that we have had negative thoughts about what other drivers are doing for some time. Every time someone drives poorly around us we allow ourselves to have these negative, violent thoughts and eventually they come out. Road rage is not an instantaneous event. It has built up over a period of time because of the habitual way we have allowed ourselves to think, and then it suddenly erupts. If we are going to address road rage we don't just look at the behavior during the incident in question, we must look at the messages we have been giving ourselves over the past weeks or months. Then we must decide on more appropriate thoughts to have and make those the habitual thoughts we have when another motorist drives poorly. This takes practice. This means developing a different thought pattern, a different set of thoughts.

Let me be clear. The habitual thoughts we have are not random, solitary events. They become what is called our internal dialogue. We have these habitual thoughts over and over and over. They become an ongoing, unending pattern of thoughts. This collection of habitual thoughts, this internal dialogue, becomes part of our belief system. It becomes part of the way we define ourselves.

> This collection of habitual thoughts, this internal
>
> dialogue, becomes part of our belief system. It
>
> becomes part of the way we define ourselves.

The habitual thoughts we have can be positive, or they can be negative. When they are negative we describe them as automatic negative thoughts(ANTS). Dr. Daniel Amen, author of *Mind Coach,* describes some common forms they can take with children. He discusses nine types of automatic negative thoughts. The first is "All or nothing thinking." This is when we think that things are either all good or all bad. There is no in between. There is no grey. Everything is either black or white. That is simply not the case in life. There are many issues we come across that have both good and bad elements. If we think that everything is either black or white we can end up making some very poor judgments and very poor decisions.

The second automatic negative thought Dr. Amen describes is "Always thinking." We think in terms like always, never, no one, everyone, every time, everything, etc. When we think like this we can easily talk ourselves into a rage because we convince ourselves that we are always being victimized, that we never get our turn, and that everyone else gets the breaks. This is both unhealthy and it produces stress.

The third automatic negative thought is "Focusing on the negative." This means we see the bad in every situation. We cannot look at the good. The bad, the negative consumes us. Ever know anyone who consistently thinks like that? They become real downers and are hard to be around for any length of time because of their negativity.

The fourth automatic negative thought is "Fortunetelling." This is where we predict the worst possible outcome for a situation. "I know I'll fail." "I know if I do this it will turn out wrong." "I know I won't get chosen for the team or get that promotion." When we think like this, when we predict the worst, that is often what we actually get. Our negative thinking influences our behavior and that influences the outcome. It becomes the inevitable self-fulfilling prophecy.

The fifth automatic negative thought is "Mind reading." This refers to knowing, or thinking we know, what other people are thinking even though they have not said it. "I know they don't like me because I'm too fat." "I know he thinks I'm stupid." "I know she won't go out with me because she thinks I'm a nerd." Again, when we think like this on a regular basis, it becomes our reality. We think someone does not like us, so we behave in a way that is unlikeable, and guess what...they end up not liking us. And we come away thinking, "I knew it all the time."

"Thinking with our feelings" is the sixth automatic negative thought. This refers to believing our negative feeling without ever questioning them. Have you ever made a mistake and you end up telling yourself something like, "I'm stupid, I'm just so stupid, I'm stupid, stupid, stupid?" In fact, making a mistake does not mean you are stupid. It may mean you were not focused or not thinking about what you were doing, but we over-react, we think with our feelings, and we feel an overwhelming failure or ineptitude. That then impacts what we do next, which may be a very poor, misguided reaction.

The seventh automatic negative thought is "Guilt beatings.". This is when we think in terms like "I should, I must, I ought, I have to." We feel like we have to behave in a certain manner, that we must do specific tasks, that others expect certain things from us and we are letting everyone down if we do not perform in the expected manner. Ever felt like that? It generates stress.

The eighth automatic negative thought is "Labeling." This is when we label ourselves or others. We make a mistake and we label ourselves as stupid. We don't do something as well as we thought we should and we label ourselves as inept. We stumble and we call ourselves clumsy, or facetiously name ourselves "Grace." When we put these labels on ourselves we tend to live up to them, because they impact our perceptions of ourselves. They impact our reality.

Dr. Amen's Nine Automatic Negative Thoughts

All or nothing thinking – Everything is all good or all bad, there is no in-between

Always thinking – Thinking in terms like always, never, no one, everyone, every time, etc.

Focusing on the negative – Always looking at the bad or the negative in everything that happens

Fortunetelling – Predicting the worst possible outcome, "I know I will fail."

Mind reading – Thinking you know what others think, and that it is negative, despite the fact you have not really checked it out

Thinking with our feelings – Believing our feelings without ever checking them out

Guilt beatings – Thinking in phrases like "I should, I must, I ought, I have to"

Labeling – Putting labels on others or on ourselves like, "I'm stupid, I'm inept, I'm clumsy"

Blame – Always finding someone or something to blame for our problems, never really accepting ownership of our actions and behaviors

Gary R. Plaford

The final automatic negative thought is "Blame." This means we blame others or blame something else for our problems. We do not take ownership of the problem. It is someone else's fault we are in this situation. The problem with always blaming someone or something else rather than taking ownership is that to control our own behavior, our own actions, we must own that behavior. If we do not take ownership, if we do not take responsibility, then we will never be able to control what happens. We cannot control our behavior until we own our behavior.

These automatic negative thoughts are habits. They are habitual ways we think about issues. As stated earlier, these automatic thoughts become part of our ongoing internal dialogue... our belief system...and ultimately part of how we define ourselves. While Dr. Amen described these as automatic thoughts children and adolescents often have, these same habitual thought patterns exist in many adults. These habits can generate a tremendous amount of stress in our lives.

Habits are interesting. They are learned behavior. The brain is a phenomenal organ in that regard. It is designed to learn, to forge neural pathways so that we can repeat behaviors. It is very good at that task. Neural pathways are developed, dendrites become bushier, and the speed of the brain's communication regarding the behavior speeds up. In other words, we learn. The problem is that the brain is not so good at unlearning. Once we have learned a behavior or a thought pattern it is difficult to just ignore it. It is difficult to try to not perform a habit. This is why habits are so hard to break. This is why the most effective way to deal with a habit is not to try to stop it, but rather to replace it with a different habit. This is true for behaviors, and it is true for habitual thought patterns.

When I lecture, one activity I often use is to have a volunteer look at colors and tell me what colors they are seeing. The goal is to tell me the colors as quickly as they can. This sounds fairly simple. However, when I hold up the colors for them to begin, the trick is that the colors are words, and they are color words. For example, the first color in the row may be "green," but it is the printed word "yellow." The next color is "red," but the word is "blue." Their task is to tell me the color they are seeing not to read the word. This becomes very difficult. They will continually read the word instead of stating the color, even though they are trying to just state the color. Why does this happen? It happens because we have the habit of looking at a word and reading the word. What I am asking them to do is look at a word and tell me the color ink it is printed in. I am asking them to act against their habit, and it is difficult.

This is often exactly what we do with children. A child misbehaves, they act improperly, and we tell them not to do that, but rather to do this. Then we expect them to act properly the next time. When the next occasion occurs they again misbehave, and we tell them they aren't trying or they weren't listening. In some instances they really were trying and they were listening, but they have habitual ways they think and we are asking them to go against their habits, and that is difficult. If we really want them to be successful we need to not only tell them how to behave but get them to practice that new behavior. In fact, they need to practice it over and over and over again to allow that to become their new habit. Then when the situation comes up again they really have a chance to behave as we would like. It is all about habits.

Have you ever gone back to visit your parents at Christmas, or Chanukah, or Thanksgiving, or some other occasion and your mother or father said something to you or did something and suddenly you were caught up into feeling and acting exactly like you did when you were a teenager? They pulled your string or hit that nerve, or whatever you want to call it. Or you go back for a family gathering and your brother or sister says or does something and suddenly you are squabbling with them just like you did when you were thirteen? Why does this happen? It is because the neural pathways we laid down back when we were living with them, the thought habits we formed long ago, are still there. They have not been replaced. So when they get triggered by a word or a deed, a comment or an action, we are right back into the old way of thinking and acting or reacting. The brain is great at forging these neural pathways for learning, for developing habits, but it is not good at unlearning them. Sometimes this is embarrassing, sometimes it becomes funny, and sometimes it is tragic, but it is a fact of how we function. Again, the best way to deal with habits of any kind is not to try to change them or ignore them or resist them, but to replace them. Replacing habits, behavioral habits or thought habits, is the best way of managing those habits.

In Summation

1. We have many habits that help us get through each and every day. Some of those are good habits and sometimes they are bad or negative habits.

2. In addition to behavioral habits we also have thought habits, the habitual way we think about issues.

3. Habitual thoughts make up our internal dialogue which becomes part of our belief system and part of how we define ourselves.

4. Thought habits can also be positive or negative.

5. Some typical negative thought habits include; all or nothing thinking, always thinking, focusing on the negative, fortunetelling, mind reading, thinking with our feelings, guilt beatings, labeling, and blaming.

6. All habits are learned behaviors. They become habits because we practice them. We develop and rehearse them and we lay the neural pathways by reinforcing them.

7. Our habits are easily triggered, hard to ignore and hard to change.

8. The best way to beat a habit is to replace it with a different habit, a different thought or action. The new thought or action must be practiced repeatedly to make sure that becomes our new habit.

PART II

Managing Stress

Introduction

What makes us who we are? We can describe the color and texture of our skin, the color of our hair, the color of our eyes, how tall we are, how much we weigh, but does that do justice to who we are? Not really. Who we really are is the culmination of our experiences, our relationships, our memories, our thoughts, our values, our desires, our will, the stresses we face and how we manage them. Ninety-nine percent of who we really are is invisible and untouchable. We can spend a lot of time creaming and smoothing our skin, coloring and cutting our hair, dieting and exercising to sculpt our bodies, but how much time do we spend on the ninety-nine percent within us that is invisible and untouchable?

How do we begin the discussion of managing stress? How do we organize it so that it makes sense? How can we make it meaningful and workable? There are numerous approaches out there. Some talk about general stress reduction techniques. Some strategies talk about reducing stressors at work and reducing stressors in our personal lives. Some strategies talk about action based strategies and perceptual based strategies.

Let me begin by pointing out that stress is not an external event. It may be initiated by an external event, but it is in itself not an external event. Stress comes from the evaluation we give events. It is how we evaluate, how we interpret, the level of importance we give such events that creates stress. Stress is an internal reaction. This is why we can create stress in our lives just with our thoughts, and this is why a specific event may cause a high level of stress in one person but only moderate or mild stress in another. It is internal.

So how do we function internally? There are various aspect that make us who we are. We have the physical side of us, the mental side of us, the emotional side, and the spiritual side. These aspects of our lives are different, yet they have significant interaction with each other. What we are going through physically certainly can affect us mentally, emotionally, and spiritually. If we are suffering through a severe illness, for example, that can affect our mental outlook, our emotional reactions, and cause us to evaluate our spiritual being. Mental issues affect us physically, emotionally, and spiritually. Emotional issues and spiritual issues can likewise affect us in all other areas. However, I believe the best way of looking at managing stress is to look at it in terms of what we can do physically, what we can do mentally, what we can do emotionally, and what we can do spiritually to address the stresses we face.

In looking at strategies in this manner some of the strategies will overlap, but I believe this is an easier way to categorize what we can do to help ourselves. When we address strategies through the physical, mental, emotional, and spiritual lens these strategies will be applicable and useful for what we face at work and in our personal lives, for both active and perceptual approaches, and for general stress reduction versus dealing with specific stressors. Consequently, in the second part of this book we will examine physical, mental, emotional, and spiritual strategies.

Physical strategies include such things as understanding and utilizing exercise, Yoga, Tai Chi, deep breathing, healthy life style, healthy diet, progressive muscle relaxation, and proper sleep. Mental strategies include such things as recognizing and avoiding stressors, learning to set goals and plan rather than merely react to issues, learning to analyze our stressors and reframe issues, looking at our coping skills and developing effective problems solving skills, addressing our mindset and self-perceptions, looking at the assumptions we make, learning to focus on the positive and positive thinking versus negativity, building self-confidence and self-esteem, utilizing techniques such as meditation, bio-feedback, imagery, and relaxation, and scheduling in a time for fun and for building and maintaining relationships. Emotional strategies include addressing the four conditions that cause stress, building emotional intelligence, learning to shift the locus of control in our brain at will, anger management, learning patience, cognitive restructuring, learning and utilizing calming techniques and cues, reframing stressors and looking at what is controllable and what is not within our control. Spiritual strategies are not merely religious in nature. These include addressing what we value, what we believe, looking at the big picture and setting preferences, examining what is really important to us, the questions we ask ourselves, and based on all that, how we utilize our time.

Having said that I must also point out that there are a multitude of strategies for managing stress cited in this part of the book. There are far too many strategies to incorporate in any one individual's life. The point of presenting so many and so varied approaches to stress management is that we are all so different, and what works for one individual will not necessarily be the best approach for another. No one could possibly incorporate every strategy cited, nor would they need to. The point here is to open our minds to the various strategies, and select those that are the most promising for us and our individual situations. Some strategies might work best in some situations, and other strategies might work better in different situations. We sometimes find as we grow in our ability to manage stress that different strategies will take on more or less significance. Additionally, as we age our strategies can change. The important thing to remember is that there are strategies that will work for each of us. Select those strategies to incorporate now, and keep this book handy as a reference for dealing with potential future stresses that might require alternative strategies.

CHAPTER 7

Physical Strategies for Managing Stress

Modern medicine, specifically pharmacology, always seems to be looking for the magic cure, the magic bullet, the pill that will make us healthy and live longer. It has fallen short in this quest. The closest thing we have to a magic bullet is exercise. Exercise improves sleep, it increases longevity, it stimulates brain cell growth, it controls weight, it improves muscle strength, it increases bone density, it lowers cholesterol, it improves cardiovascular health, it lowers blood pressure, it prevents diabetes, and it lowers the risk of stroke. If exercise were a prescription drug it would undoubtedly be the most widely prescribed medication in the world.

In this chapter we will discuss physical strategies for managing and lowering stress. Physical strategies include such things as exercise, Yoga, Tai Chi, deep breathing, healthy life style, healthy diet, progressive muscle relaxation, and proper sleep.

Exercise

First and foremost, exercise plays a critical role in managing stress. When we are experiencing high levels of stress our bodies are preparing for, or already in, what is called fight or flight mode. Levels of cortisol, often referred to as the stress hormone, have increased. Levels of serotonin, which is one of the calming/feel good hormones, have decreased. We are primed for action. The body is ready for action, fight or flight, and it is calling for action. The best thing to do is to give it action, to exercise. As human beings we did not evolve to sit in front of a television, we evolved to move. So when we are stressed we should not sit in front of a television, we need to move our bodies.

When we exercise it accomplishes a number of things. First of all exercise reduces anxiety. Studies have proven that nervous tension and hyperactivity decrease when we exercise. Exercise relaxes us. It calms the nerves, it slows us down. Stress speeds us up. Stress kicks in our sympathetic nervous response. This is like putting one's foot down on the gas pedal of a car, we go faster. Exercise helps kick in the parasympathetic nervous response, it slows us down. It is like stepping on the brakes. Exercise also makes us feel better, and even feel better about ourselves. It lifts our mood, it makes us feel more optimistic about tomorrow and we feel better about ourselves because we worked out.

The thought at the beginning of this chapter mentions a number of benefits from exercise, but how does exercising accomplish these benefits? First of all, exercise increases oxygen flow. All the cells in the body, including the brain, require oxygen. In fact, although the brain makes up only two to three percent of our body mass, it uses from fifteen-twenty percent of the oxygen we breathe into our lungs. All of our cells use oxygen to metabolize energy. Without this they cease function. Exercise is the quickest way to generate higher levels of oxygen to the brain and other cells, and we think better and function better as a result. When we are mentally fatigued and are not thinking well, a little exercise will pick us up and boost our thought processes.

Exercise also reduces the tension in our muscles. Have you ever noticed that when you are stressed your back or neck tightens up? Exercise reduces that tension and hence relaxes us. In fact, when we are tense the body generates toxic waste which we need to eliminate from the body. Some of this toxin can actually be reduced by sweating it out.

Exercise, and the deeper breathing that goes with it, also has a positive and necessary effect on the lymphatic system. The lymphatic system moves cellular fluid from the cells and eventually to the circulatory system. This fluid contains waste product from cells among other things, which must be eliminated from the body. When the lymphatic system does not work properly we can have swelling, as when someone's ankles or feet swell. The lymphatic system, unlike the circulatory system, has no pump. The circulatory system has a pump, the heart, which moves blood through the body. The lymphatic system, without such a pump, requires movement of the body to accomplish this. Hence, exercise helps the lymphatic system to function properly.

Exercise also improves metabolism. The body will burn calories more efficiently when we exercise thus helping to maintain weight. Being sedentary causes the body to store calories as fat rather than burn them, which means added pounds we carry around. This increases both our physical stress and our mental stress.

Additionally, exercise raises our endorphin levels. Endorphins are neurotransmitters that make us feel good. Not only does this improve our mood, but it gives us a better outlook for the future. A part of feeling better includes the fact that exercising gets the focus of our thoughts off the problems that are stressing us out in the first place. That also lifts our mood and calms us.

Finally, exercise improves the quality of our sleep, which has a tremendous effect on stress. I will talk more about sleep later, but exercise causes the body temperature to elevate. When we have a good work out our body temperature will rise and remain elevated for two to four hours after working out. Then it drops. Body temperature fluctuations are one of the keys for sleeping well. We sleep better when the body temperature falls. With people who sleep well, the body temperature drop is part of what helps them attain sleep. With people diagnosed with insomnia the body temperature drops several hours later than it does with "good sleepers," and for insomniacs the range of temperature change is also diminished. Exercise helps to establish or re-establish this temperature fluctuation.

With all that we know about exercise it is clear that it can play a critical factor in reducing stress in our lives. What is important, therefore, is to get out there and exercise regularly. This means we must find a way to exercise that we can live with. If we hate it, it will be difficult to keep doing it. But exercising does not have to be something we hate. Finding something that we can do with others is a good place to begin. This could include playing tennis, playing golf and walking the course, or simply walking. Walking at least a half hour every day is a wonderful exercise. We can then gradually increase the length of time and the pace. It is important to start slow and build up gradually. If we overdo it initially, if we have sore muscles and pain form doing it, chances are we won't go out and do it again tomorrow. It is also important to make the exercise as interesting as we can. This means varying the workout. If it is a walk, we can vary where we walk, or find others to walk with. The important thing is to do it consistently. Make exercise a habit, a way of life.

Yoga

Granted, yoga is a form of exercise. However, I wanted to discuss it a little more specifically. Practicing yoga not only reduces anxiety, but it creates a mind-body balance. Hatha yoga puts the body into postures that stretch it beyond its normal limits. This can relieve mild aches and pains throughout the body, back pain, and even menstrual cramps. The deep breathing and concentration techniques that go along with the postures calm the mind and increase blood flow throughout the body and brain. Yoga is calming. It slows us down. It lowers blood pressure and heart rate. It is a wonderful tool to use in addressing anger or other negative emotions as well as lowering stress. Yoga is a good tool to teach children because it gives them control over negative emotions, so that when they become upset they can be reminded to use their yoga postures to regain control emotionally.

Tai Chi

Like yoga, Tai Chi is obviously an exercise. While yoga utilizes poses that are taken and held, Tai Chi uses fluid motions to and through specific poses. It does not stop at a pose, but rather is a continuous slow journey through multiple poses and positions. Tai Chi is considered a martial art, but is deflective rather than aggressive in nature. It connects the mind and body, and like yoga, is a wonderful tool for reducing stress.

Deep Breathing

Deep breathing is another great tool for lowering stress. Many people breathe shallowly. They breathe with their chests only. This is especially true when we are stressed. When we are stressed we often resort to quick shallow breaths, while breathing more deeply is really what we should do. Deep breathing is sometimes called stomach breathing, abdominal breathing, belly breathing, or diaphragmatic breathing. When we induce deep breathing the diaphragm actually moves down when we inhale and back up when we exhale. The diaphragm supports the organs above it, which include the heart and the lungs. The more deeply we inhale the further down the diaphragm moves. Since the lungs are actually larger at the bottom than the top, this allows them to use their full structure and take in more oxygen. Hence the oxygen-carbon dioxide exchange becomes greater.

Additionally, this fuller range of movement of the diaphragm massages the organs below the diaphragm. This includes the liver, kidneys, spleen, etc. This massaging motion, as with exercise, helps move lymphatic fluid through the lymphatic system. This is crucial for getting rid of cellular waste, aiding in the absorption of fatty acids, and also plays an important role in moving lymphocytes and monocytes that play a key role in our immune system. Additionally, the slow, rhythmic movement created by deep breathing helps to engage the parasympathetic nervous system. As stated before, the sympathetic nervous system revs us up, the parasympathetic system slows us down.

Healthy Lifestyle

Having a healthy lifestyle includes such things as exercising, maintaining a healthy diet, getting proper sleep...issues that are discussed separately in this section. However, a healthy lifestyle also means not doing things to the brain and body that have negative effects. This would include such things as smoking cigarettes. We are all aware of the cancer risks from smoking or other forms of using tobacco, and we are aware of the risks for issues like emphysema. These risks are well documented. However, nicotine also elevates stress hormones. By doing so it accelerates the heart rate, and the breathing rate. Nicotine also speeds up brain waves. These factors have a very detrimental effect on both sleep and stress. Brain waves have to slow down for us to sleep, not speed up. Heart rhythms and breathing rhythms also have to decrease if we are to attain good sleep. For an individual addicted to nicotine a cigarette has an immediate calming effect because it reduces the craving, but in the long run it has the effect of creating higher levels of stress.

Good lifestyle choices also involve the use of caffeine. Caffeine is a stimulant. Many people with insomnia use caffeine to keep them going through the day. They do not sleep well at night so they are tired and drowsy during the day, so they drink coffee or use high energy drinks to keep functioning. Then at night, of course, they don't sleep well. It becomes a vicious cycle. Caffeine has a half-life of about eight hours. This means that it is still in your system after eight hours, although the effects will have mostly worn off. This means that if we go to bed at ten o'clock at night, any caffeine that we used after two o'clock that afternoon, e.g., that four o'clock cup of coffee or energy drink, can still disrupt our ability to sleep.

Some people have such a powerful drive to sleep (which will be discussed momentarily when we discuss sleep) that caffeine use does not seem to affect them. Those people need to be aware, however, that as the body ages it metabolizes caffeine more slowly and at some point in time it might affect their sleep. The point is, if we use caffeine, and I love my morning coffee as well as the next person, we need to use it wisely. That means, for most of us, don't use caffeine after two o'clock in the afternoon. Not using caffeine after two o'clock in the afternoon not only means curtailing the consumption of coffee, tea, colas, or most high energy drinks...it also means looking at the caffeine levels of other substances we ingest. This includes some foods, chocolates, and specifically headache remedies. Some of the over the counter medications we take have high levels of caffeine in them. If they do, and caffeine intake is a problem, the best solution is to try to find alternatives.

Another lifestyle choice involves the use of alcohol. Although alcohol was once prescribed by some physicians for sleep, it actually has the opposite effect. While alcohol can help people nod off earlier, the problems occur later in the sleep cycle with the result of not being able to stay asleep. One of the reasons for this is that alcohol disrupts REM sleep. While we sleep in ninety minute cycles and get some of each sleep stage in every one of these cycles, most of our REM sleep comes in the later cycles. In other words, the first three to four hours of sleep will be spent getting mostly deep sleep and the last three or so hours will be spent more in REM sleep. But if REM sleep is being disrupted, then instead of getting that good REM sleep, we wake up. This is what happens when we drink alcohol too late in the evening or in too much excess, we wake up half way through the night and cannot get back to sleep. We are not getting enough REM sleep when this happens. One night of this may not be so bad, but if it becomes a pattern we will begin to have problems. Additionally, alcohol has a diuretic effect, meaning that we will need to get up to use the bathroom, and once we get up to use the bathroom it becomes difficult to get back to sleep. Finally, alcohol is a muscle relaxant. Again, this may aid in getting to sleep initially, but problems occur when the muscles in the throat relax. When that occurs the air way is smaller, breathing becomes more difficult and we snore. In some cases the oxygen restriction causes or worsens sleep apnea. With either heavy snoring or sleep apnea the amount of oxygen taken into the lungs decreases which can result in either heart disease or a heart attack, and it results in staying in the lighter stages of sleep which means not getting as much deep sleep or REM sleep. All of these issues negatively impact sleep and increase our level of stress.

Lifestyle choices also include the use of drugs, which includes both recreational drugs and prescription drugs. Marijuana and cocaine, for example, both restrict REM sleep. Hence they will have the same effect as alcohol on disrupting that stage of sleep and the consequences when that occurs. Also, some prescription drugs decrease REM sleep, so it is important to know the effect these drugs will have on us before we agree to take things on any long term basis.

A healthy lifestyle also includes having fun and relaxation as part of our lives. Taking a vacation is a great way to get away from stressors and relax. But merely planning a vacation can be fun and relaxing too. When we plan for a vacation we begin looking at the place we're going and the things we will do there, and we begin to imagine the fun we will have. The actual vacation will be limited by the amount of time we have to spend on vacation, but the planning of it can go on for long periods and can bring us a lot of enjoyment and stress relief in the planning and imagining we do.

As fun and relaxing as vacations can be, we cannot limit the fun in our lives to vacation time. We need to enjoy life today, and every day. This means finding things we enjoy and working time for those things into the schedule. It also means working in some relaxation after work. Take fifteen or twenty minutes to go for a walk, or to sit and do deep breathing or yoga, or take that time to read a book. This time, although brief, will help us wind down and relax. It becomes a trigger for the mind and body that the stress of the day is set aside, even if only briefly. When we are stressed about our day we remain focused on the issues of our day, but when we relax we take the time to notice and appreciate the wonders and the beauty that is around us in the little things. This is a measure of the quality of our life. As long as we breathe in and out we are technically alive. But "being alive" and "living life" are really two separate things. Only when we have achieved both of these can we truly be fulfilled.

The final lifestyle issue I want to mention concerns television and the amount of time spent watching television. In our hectic lives we all need some down time, some time that we don't have to really think, some time to "veg out." Watching television can certainly fill that time. However, many people are spending incredible amounts of time watching television. We were not evolved to have that much down time. Too much time watching television becomes very detrimental and, in fact, a health hazard. We can become too sedentary, and that increases the stress level because we are not working the stress out, and we are also typically gaining weight because of the inactivity. Besides the lack of physical activity brought about by spending too much time in front of the television, there is the lack of mental activity. Television watching is both physically and mentally passive. Reading a book is physically passive but mentally active. There is a huge difference.

A final issue I need to discuss regarding television concerns blue light. This requires some explanation. In 2001 it was discovered that we have receptors in the eyes that do not feed to the occipital cortex, the visual center of the brain, but rather to the hypothalamus, and specifically to an area of the hypothalamus called the suprachiasmatic neucleus. This is the area of the brain commonly referred to as the biological clock. This keeps our circadian cycle functioning in rhythm. This area drops our body temperature during the night and raises it during the day, which is a huge part of being able to sleep.

The fact that these light receptors in the eye feed to this area is how we know whether it is daylight or night, and thus how the brain knows whether to turn on these daylight functions or the night time functions. Specifically it is blue light that the brain perceives as daylight. Natural sunlight, and most light from average light bulbs would be called white light. White light is made up of all the spectrum of light wave lengths. Red wave lengths are the longest, then orange, yellow, green, etc. The blue to violet wavelengths are the shortest. We can see the wavelengths separated when we see a rainbow, or when we look at light that is filtered through a prism. These shortest wavelengths, the blue to violet, are what the brain perceives as daylight.

Gary R. Plaford

Blue light is present in natural light, but it is highly prevalent in most television screens, computer screens, and cell phone screens. Hence, when we watch television we are getting a lot of blue light, which means we are signaling the brain that it is daylight. If we watch television up until the time we go to bed, then we are signaling the brain that it is daylight until we go to bed. When we get into bed and lie there unable to get to sleep, even though we might be tired, we wonder why we cannot drop into sleep. For those who have this problem, the key is to stop watching television an hour or two before going to bed. For those who will not do that there are some other strategies that will be discussed shortly regarding how to improve sleep, but understand that a major problem with many people and sleep is the high infusion of blue light right up until bedtime.

Healthy Diet

Another physical strategy for reducing stress is to eat a healthy diet. First of all, the calories that we take into our body are burned as fuel, hence fueling our daily activity. Optimally we burn the number of calories that we take in. When there is a discrepancy in this we either gain weight or lose weight. When we take in more that we burn, the body stores the excess as fat. When we take in less than we burn the body will burn some of the fat we have stored. There are factors that cause the body and brain to burn more or less calories, and hence store or burn excess fat, but basically the formula is we take in calories, we burn calories, and then we deal with the excesses. With that said, the tendency to "supersize" our servings has a very detrimental impact on health and hence on stress levels. Quantity is important.

The quality of the diet is also important. The faster pace of our society as well as the ability to both produce and distribute products everywhere has made fast food and snack food viable choices in our caloric consumption. But fast foods and snack foods are not necessarily healthy. In fact let's leave out the "necessarily." Fast foods and snack foods are not healthy, and especially not healthy if they are the mainstay of our diets. These foods typically contain high quantities of sugars and high quantities of fats. It is so easy to gain weight eating these foods regularly. This added weight increases the physical stress on our bodies. The gradual deterioration of physical health also adds stress. Then the fact that we cannot get into our favorite jeans adds mental stress. This book is in no way a diet book, but the way we eat, the quantity and quality of food we ingest, can have a significant impact on the level of stress we have in our lives. Additionally, as Michael Breus points out in his book, *The Sleep Doctor's Diet Plan,* weight gain and weight loss are intricately related to sleep.

Sleep

Sleep is inexorably linked to stress, and stress is likewise linked to sleep. When we do not sleep well it elevates our stress level. We are more irritable, we don't handle frustration well, we snap more easily at others, and on and on. When we are stressed we don't sleep well. We cannot get to sleep, the mind keeps replaying the issues that are stressing us out, and once we do fall asleep we wake up in the middle of the night worrying and cannot get back to sleep. A major strategy in managing sleep is to reduce stress, and a major strategy to reduce stress is to improve the quantity and quality of sleep. So how can we improve sleep? As I discussed in a previous book, *Sleep and Learning,* the first step in improving sleep is to address the senses including vision, hearing, touch, taste, and smell.

Vision is a critical piece of the puzzle. Light plays a major role in the sleep equation; in fact it is blue light that is interpreted as daylight by the brain. There has been some recent and interesting research done about the effects of blue light. One such study was done by N. Santhi, et.al, entitled "The spectral composition of evening light and individual differences in the suppression of melatonin and delay of sleep in humans." We have already discussed blue light in regard to television watching. The light that enters our eyes acts as a signal to the brain, specifically the hypothalamus and the biological clock, that it is daylight. The hypothalamus in turn begins to elevate our body temperature, and this wakes us up. Hence when we get too much light, specifically blue light, right before bed we are signaling the brain that it is daylight. This has a negative effect on our ability to then get to sleep. Some people argue that they go to bed watching the television and that helps put them to sleep. They may be able to go to sleep that way, because the drive for sleep is so strong that the body craves sleep and will put us into sleep, but what happens is that they also will tend to wake up more during the night. They cannot stay asleep because of body temperature elevation.

We sleep best when our body temperature drops several degrees. Body temperature has been measured during sleep, and for someone with a waking body temperature of 98.6 degrees their temperature at its low point during the night may be 96 degrees... a drop of 2.6 degrees. In Dr. Gregg Jacobs book, *Say Good Night To Insomnia,* he points out that people with insomnia have various issues in regard to body temperature. First, their body temperature begins to drop several hours later than a "sound sleeper." This is part of the reason they cannot get to sleep. Secondly, their body temperature does not drop as much as a "good sleeper." This is why they often cannot stay asleep during the night. Body temperature is a critical part of getting to sleep and remaining asleep, and the light that enters our eyes plays a key role in regulating that body temperature.

The bottom line is that too much light the last hour or so before bed, which especially includes light from television and computer screens because of the high concentration of blue light, can derail our ability to either go to sleep or stay asleep. The other end of the spectrum is also important. Because light elevates the body temperature and wakes us up, it is important to get enough blue light in the morning. Getting plenty of morning light will help reset the biological clock and it will then be easier to get to sleep at night. So the simple rules is, get out in the sunlight each and every morning and limit the light we allow ourselves the last several hours before bed.

The best way to limit night time light is to stop watching television, get off the computer, and stop texting on your cell phone the last several hours before bed. Dim the lights and read a book with a light that shines only on the book pages. If you cannot read before bed then listen to quiet music in the dim light, take a warm bath in candle light, etc. If you simply must watch television up until the time for bed, then purchase some sunglasses that have a high yellow content, such as Blueblockers, and wear those the last two hours of television watching. Highly tinted yellow sunglasses will block out blue light. If we can block out about ninety-five percent of the blue light the brain will not interpret it as daylight and it won't have such a negative effect on sleep.

Another issue with light is the importance of sleeping in darkness. Make sure the bedroom is really dark. Darkness promotes the release of melatonin, and the release of melatonin helps us get to sleep and remain asleep. This impacts not merely getting to sleep but the level of sleep we attain. We don't merely need sleep; we need the right amount of both deep sleep and REM sleep. Deep sleep is critical, and I truly mean critical for health reasons. REM sleep is equally critical for both memory and mental health reasons. Even if we sleep long enough, but it is mainly stage two non-REM sleep instead of enough of the deep sleep and REM sleep, then we will still have problems.

In his book, *A Good Night's Sleep,* Dr. Lawrence Epstein discusses various issues around shift work, including the fact that night shift workers experience higher incidents of heart disease, cancer, diabetes, etc. The reason for this is sleep, or rather lack of sleep. Many such workers do not sleep in total darkness, which means they are not getting sufficient melatonin release, which means they are not getting enough deep sleep or REM sleep. It is truly important for night shift workers to either sleep in a room without windows or get black out curtains that really block out the light for when they do sleep.

Besides the light issue, vision also plays a role in sleep because of what we see. Having clutter in the bedroom has a negative impact on our sleep. Having a computer in the bedroom will remind us of the work that we need to do, the email we need to answer, the paper we need to write, the issue we need to check out on the internet, etc. These things start the mind racing, and sometimes we cannot turn it off, and we cannot get to sleep. Wearing eye shades can block out light as well as clutter.

Hearing is another sense that can either help or hinder sleep. Most of us have had the experience of listening to a dog bark endlessly during the night. Those experiences are maddening because we don't sleep well through that noise. If it is our own dog it is bad enough, but when the dog belongs to a neighbor. The point is, noise impacts our ability to sleep. This is another reason not to have the television on when we go to bed. The sound may help us get to sleep, but eventually that same sound will wake us up at one thirty in the morning. Not to mention the fact that even if we go to sleep during a program we like, the commercials are programed at a higher volume level so they will do their part in waking us up. If you must go to sleep with the television on, at least set a timer so it will turn off at a specific time.

Better than television is music. However, the music needs to be something slow and soft and repetitive. Vocals are not good because we can get caught up in the lyrics that start the mind racing. Anything that changes beat, or volume, or tempo is also bad for sleeping. That includes most rock music, heavy metal music, or rap. If it is for sleep, the music needs to be soft, consistent, and repetitive. This would be more like yoga, massage, or meditation music. Another strategy to address hearing is to use a white noise machine. These use either the sounds of water, nature, or just soft static to block out other sounds. The use of ear plugs can also be helpful. A strategy I especially like is using a progressive muscle relaxation CD. In this type of CD the voice softly and quietly talks us through relaxing each part of the body. It suggests we first tighten the muscles in our feet, hold them tight, and then finally relax the feet. Then we go to the calves and do the same. Gradually we have relaxed every part of the body. The sound of the voice is a huge part of that relaxation. The actual muscle relaxation leads us into a discussion of the next sense.

The sense of touch or feel plays a critical role in sleep. As just mentioned, a progressive muscle relaxation CD is a wonderful tool to have in our sleep arsenal. Relaxing the muscles makes us feel so much better that it enables sleep to come. When the muscles in any part of our body are tense it is much harder to fall asleep. Hence progressive muscle relaxation is beneficial. We can also utilize a little stretching before bed. Again, this loosens us up, stretches and relaxes the muscles, and relieves tightness. Getting a massage before bed can also be very relaxing. If we cannot get someone else to provide the massage, then massaging the parts of our own body that are tense can help. Massaging the tightness out of our calves or neck can do wonders.

The sense of touch also encompasses being clean and having clean sheets or pillowcases to sleep on. It also means being clean ourselves. Going to bed after a bath or shower helps the body to feel better and will aid in sleep. Having a little something on the stomach can aid sleep. Having nothing on the stomach, that sense of hunger, can keep us awake, but having too much on the stomach, being full, can also disrupt sleep. The ambient temperature we sleep in also affects how we sleep. Some of us remember back before the days of air conditioning when some summer nights where just too hot to sleep. Most people actually sleep best when the room temperature is somewhere around 69 degrees. That varies a little, but that is a good place to start with the thermostat when we are having sleep issues. Another helpful tip, for those who wake up during the night and have trouble getting back to sleep, is to cool your body down and then go back to sleep. In the winter this is easy, simply step out on the back porch for a few minutes. Really cool yourself down, and then go back to bed. The combination of cooling the body down and then the wonderful feel of the cozy bed will help you get back to sleep. A cold shower is also effective. There are even temperature control mattress pads that allow for setting the temperature at a low enough level to both get to sleep more easily and remain asleep better throughout the night.

The sense of taste does not play as significant a role as the other senses, but it is still important enough to address. Having a bad taste in the mouth can deter sleep. Likewise spicy hot sensations or a lingering sweetness can disrupt our ability to fall asleep. The best thing to do is make sure you brush your teeth well before bed to get rid of unwelcome, sleep-detracting tastes.

Tips for Using the Senses to Aid Sleep

Vision – Get plenty of sunlight in the morning, limit blue light before bed, stop watching television an hour before bed or use Blueblocker sunglasses the last hour, sleep in darkness, remove clutter like computers from the bedroom.

Hearing – Don't go to bed watching television, listen to soft music, listen to a sleep CD, utilize white noise to block out random noise, use ear plugs.

Touch – Relax the muscles with a sleep CD, stretch, massage sore muscles, wash linens, bathe, have a light snack, set the thermostat to keep you cool, use a mattress pad that keeps the temperature lower, cool your body down after night awakenings.

Taste – Brush your teeth before bed, and watch what you eat before bed.

Smell – Address unpleasant odors in the bedroom, use aroma therapy with scented candles, oils, or incense.

The sense of smell is the final sense we must address. Acrid odors can really detract from our ability to fall asleep. Something foul smelling, smelling of mildew, or smelling of old sweat like a locker room can really make it difficult to fall asleep. Addressing the foul odors is important. Also aroma therapy can be helpful. Using scented candles, oils, or incense can aid in helping us sleep.

It is important to understand that the sense of smell feeds directly to the limbic system, which is the emotional part of the brain. The other senses feed to the neo-cortex, the thinking part of the brain. The reason the sense of smell feeds to the limbic system is that it is closely linked to the fight or flight response, much more so than other senses. For example, if we see smoke it does not necessarily put us into fight or flight mode. We may see it from a long way off and wonder what is burning, but we are not necessarily concerned. If we smell smoke, however, it is close. Now we must act. We begin to wonder is the house is on fire, or other scenarios. The point is, we act. We now have to know where the smoke is coming from and are we in danger? Likewise, if we are hiking in the mountains and we see a grizzly bear on the next ridge over, it does not initiate the fight or flight response. It would take hours for the bear to descend into the valley and come back up our side of the ridge. If, however, we smell a grizzly bear we had better act immediately because we are in danger. The sense of smell can initiate our fight or flight response immediately because if we are close enough to smell danger, then we are close enough to be harmed by that danger. The issue is that the sense of smell can trigger the fight or flight response very rapidly. It can trigger a stress response in us, and that stress response is going to inhibit sleep. We cannot underestimate the importance of addressing the sense of smell.

Besides the senses there are other methods of improving sleep. The first would be to practice good sleep hygiene. This includes having a set time we go to bed at night and a set time we get up in the morning. This gets us into a routine or a rhythm and makes it easier to actually fall asleep at night. One of the common issues people have is Sunday night insomnia. For those who work or go to school Monday through Friday, this means on Sunday evening they cannot seem to get to sleep. It isn't necessarily the stress of Monday that is keeping them up, it is the fact that they slept late on Saturday and maybe even Sunday morning. This change in routine alters the body's temperature fluctuation rhythm and makes it more difficult to get to sleep. Added to that is the fact that when we sleep late one day and try to go to bed at the normal time that night, it has been a shorter time since we slept and the drive for slow wave sleep is not as intense. This also keeps us awake. The best thing to do to avoid Sunday evening insomnia is to get up on Saturday and Sunday at the same time we get up through the week. And when we get up in the morning get out in the sunlight. This will keep the body on a schedule and will aid sleep.

Besides having a routine time to go to bed and get up, sleep hygiene means having a routine for going to bed. Dim the lights an hour before bedtime. Then spend twenty minutes preparing for tomorrow, twenty minutes in bed time preparation (brushing teeth, putting on pajamas, etc.), then spend twenty minutes relaxing the mind and body. This could mean reading, listening to music, or meditating. This is quiet time. Having such a routine will begin to be a cue for the body that sleep is coming. Once we are then actually in bed, sleep will come sooner. An important fact to keep in mind is that while we can force wakefulness, we cannot force sleep. In other words, when we are sleepy we can force ourselves to remain awake, but when we are not sleepy we cannot force ourselves to go to sleep. Instead we must do things to allow sleep to come, and avoid things that will derail our ability to sleep.

Avoiding things that keep us awake would include not drinking caffeine after two o'clock in the afternoon. The effects of caffeine can last up to eight hours for most people so, as stated earlier, no caffeine after two o'clock is a good rule. Also we should not drink alcohol within three hours of bedtime. Alcohol leaves the body more quickly than caffeine, but it still requires several hours to metabolize alcohol. Additionally, don't solve or think about major problems or major decisions an hour before bed. Do that earlier and then get the mind off those issues. Those issues will keep the mind racing and derail our ability to fall asleep. Finally, although exercise is great, do not exercise during the evening right before going to bed. Exercise elevates body temperature and if we do it before bed it will keep us awake.

Some other tips for improving sleep would be to stop playing games with the snooze button on the alarm. Some people set the alarm before they actually need to get up so they can hit it a few times and lounge in bed. While this may feel good, it actually decreases the amount of actual sleep we are getting. If we set the alarm for thirty minutes before we really need to get up so we can hit the snooze button two or three times, that is actually two and a half hours a week more sleep we could be getting per week. We would feel more rested if we actually got that extra sleep. Another tip is to write down the issues that are bothering us. Keep pen and paper beside the bed. Then when we awake in the middle of the night with a pressing problem on our mind, we can sit up and write it down. Then we can literally and figuratively set it aside until tomorrow. Yet another tip is to get out of bed when we cannot sleep. If we have been laying there for over twenty minutes and we are not asleep, we should get out of bed and do something relaxing. A little while later come back and again try to get to sleep. Keep in mind that we cannot force sleep.

For some people the issue is that their sleep/wake cycle is not in sync with their sleep/work schedule. When this is the case the best thing to do is to adjust the sleep/wake cycle. We can shift the sleep/wake cycle with the use of light. Determine the time we need to get up in the morning. Then determine the time we need to go to bed to make that happen. That is the goal. Then we must get out of bed at the designated time every day, including weekends. When we get out of bed in the morning we need to make a conscious effort to get into bright sunlight for at least fifteen to twenty minutes. Avoid bright light before bed time. If the issue is that we are going to bed too early and then rising too early in the morning, we can use bright light at night before bed to stay awake longer. Melatonin can also be used to help adjust the biological clock sleep/wake cycle, but it needs to be timed properly...and melatonin should not be used by children or adolescents. It can potentially cause problems for a child's developing reproductive system.

Another strategy for improving sleep is to improve sleep efficiency. This is also discussed thoroughly in *Say Good Night to Insomnia*. Dr. Jacobs states that improving sleep efficiency is done by determining the time we go to bed, the time we get out of bed, and the time we actually were asleep while in bed. If, for example, we were in bed for eight hours but only slept about six hours, then our sleep efficiency is six over eight, or seventy-five percent. The goal would be to have a sleep efficiency of near ninety percent. So if we are getting up at six o'clock in the morning and only actually sleeping about six hours, we would go to bed at eleven forty-five at night. This allows for the six hours we are getting of sleep plus an extra fifteen minute cushion. Additionally, we only want to get into bed when we are drowsy. Going to bed at eleven forty-five instead of possibly ten o'clock should help that drowsiness. Maintaining this schedule for a week should begin to increase sleep efficiency, meaning we are actually sleeping more of the time we are in bed. Once that begins to happen we can push the bedtime forward by fifteen minutes or so. Now we are going to bed at eleven thirty. Eventually we will move the bedtime to eleven fifteen, then eleven o'clock, then ten forty five, etc. Eventually we will be sleeping more efficiently and getting the amount of sleep we require rather than lying in bed wishing we could sleep.

Another strategy to boost sleep is to simply take a nap. A nap allows us to catch up on some of the sleep we have lost. Having said that, it is important to use naps wisely. To do that it is critical to understand just a little about how we progress through the stages of sleep and the forces that drive sleep. Dr. Sara Mednick discusses this in her book, *Take a Nap! Change Your Life.*

There are five stages of sleep; stages one, two, three, and four of non-REM sleep, and REM sleep. When we first begin to sleep we go into stage one non-REM, which is basically a preparation for sleep. It is light and we only spend one to five minutes in this stage. Then we move into stage two. Brain waves begin to slow down, the body temperature begins to drop, and glucose is added to the neural sheathing around the neurons during this stage. We spend ten to fifteen minutes in stage two the first time we enter it. Then we move into stages three and four, or deep sleep, then back through a shorter stage two, and then into REM. (Some scientists are now combining stages three and four into one stage calling it all stage three. This one stage is still termed slow wave sleep or deep sleep.) This entire process takes about ninety minutes. We sleep in ninety minute segments. The important point for our purposes right at this moment, however, is to understand that when we first enter sleep we spend one to five minutes in stage one and then ten to fifteen minutes in stage two before we ever get any deep sleep or REM sleep. So roughly the first twenty minutes of sleep are stages one and two. I'll come back to this point in a moment.

The second factor to consider is that of the forces that drive sleep. The first is the need for slow wave or deep sleep. This is a powerful force. This is why we nod off even when we are trying to stay awake. This happens sometimes when we are watching television or reading a book. Unfortunately this also happens sometimes when we are driving a car late at night. We are struggling to remain awake, yet we sometimes cannot do so. This is a powerful force. The second force that drives sleep is the circadian cycle, which dictates our need for REM sleep.

When we awaken in the morning, assuming we have slept fairly well and are not suffering sleep deprivation, then the drive for slow wave sleep has been sated and is fairly low. This drive rises all day long, until at night we are again becoming drowsy and it is trying to put us to sleep. The need for REM sleep, however, is still very high when we awaken in the morning. This is when we are getting most of our REM sleep, and if we manage to sleep a little longer in the morning we will spend that extra time mostly in REM sleep. The point is, the need for slow wave sleep is low when we first awaken and the need for slow wave sleep rises throughout the day. The need for REM sleep is high when we first awaken but it drops throughout the day until late at night when it rises again. These two forces cross during the day. For someone who wakes around six in the morning and goes to bed at ten at night, these forces will cross somewhere in the early afternoon, typically between noon and two o'clock.

However, what happens when we nap? If we nap for only twenty minutes, sometimes called a power nap, we spend those twenty minute in stages one and two. This means we do not get any slow wave or REM sleep and this will have no impact on our ability to get to sleep at night. A twenty minute nap does not affect the drive for slow wave sleep. However, if we nap for an hour what happens? We will spend the first twenty minutes or so in stage one and two, but then we will get some slow wave sleep and possibly some REM sleep. This, however, will be determined by when we nap. If, for example, these forces cross around one o'clock in the afternoon and we nap several hours before they cross, then the need for REM sleep will still be greater than the need for slow wave sleep and we will spend a large part of that time in REM sleep and very little in slow wave sleep. If, however, we nap for an hour around four o'clock in the afternoon, well after these two forces have crossed, then the need for slow wave sleep is more powerful and we will spend more of that hour in slow wave and very little if any in REM. A nap at this time will definitely impact the drive for slow wave sleep and will make it much harder to then get to sleep that evening.

The point is, when we nap and how long we nap are critical factors in determining what that nap will accomplish for us. Long, late afternoon naps will disrupt our ability to go to sleep at night. Mid-morning naps won't have quite that much effect on nighttime sleeping. A twenty minute nap will have no affect at all. We can always incorporate a twenty minute nap to help us feel better and function better without disrupting our night time sleep.

A final strategy is to keep a sleep diary or journal. A sleep diary along with some general questions about sleep follows in the next several pages. Keeping such a diary for two to three weeks should give us a perspective on the issues that we might be having with sleep.

After keeping the diary for several weeks it is important to go back to what we have written down and see what is actually happening. These are then the issues we need to specifically address to improve our sleep. An explanation of the issues included in the diary includes;

1. What did you do the last two hours before going to bed? In other words are you preparing for bed or are you doing things that will keep you awake, like exercise or watching television? A strict bedtime routine prepares the mind and body for sleep.

2. What did you eat and/or drink the last two hours before bed? Again, is this something that will aid sleep or diminish sleep, and by this we mean not only getting to sleep but remaining asleep through the night?

3. What time did you go to bed? Do you have a regular bedtime or is it varied? If you are having trouble sleeping then a regular, consistent bedtime will help considerably.

4. How long did it take you to fall asleep? If this is a problem you may need to get out of bed and go to bed only when you are drowsy. The goal is to improve sleep efficiency.

5. How many times did you wake up during the night? Is night awakening the problem? If so, then addressing that by stopping alcohol consumption before bed might help, or making the effort to cool down your body temperature before returning to bed.

6. What thoughts were you having when you woke up? Is the mind racing? Keep a pen and paper by the bed and write down the troubling issues then set them aside until tomorrow. Also learning to meditate is helpful for this issue.

7. What did you do when you woke up during the night? Do you lay there and worry, or do you make the effort to get the issues out of your mind? If you lay there for longer than fifteen to twenty minutes it is better to get out of bed, get your mind off the issues, and go back to bed later.

8. Overall, how many hours did you sleep? Knowing how many hours you actually slept compared to how many hours you were in bed gives you an idea of your sleep efficiency. Poor sleep efficiency can be addressed by using a technique called Sleep Restriction Therapy. This technique requires that you determine how much time you are currently sleeping (e.g. 5 hours), then determining what time you must get out of bed in the morning (e.g. 6 o'clock), then determining when to go to bed to get that amount of sleep. In this case you would need to be in bed by 1 o'clock plus 15 minutes, so you would go to bed at 12:45 P.M. You must continue to go to bed and get up at these times every morning. When you are sleeping most of this time (at least eighty-five percent of this time) you can add another 15 minutes to your bedtime. In other words, you now go to bed at 12:30 P.M. You continue this process until you are getting 7-8 hours of sleep a night.

9. Did you wake up earlier than you expected? If you are consistently waking early then you can delay the time you go to bed by using bright light exposure before bedtime to delay drowsiness and readjust your circadian cycle.

10. What time did you get up for the day? Again, if there are sleep issues, then having a regular time to get up is critical. This will help the bedtime routine.

Sleep Diary	Day ____	Day ____	Day ____	Day ____	Day ____
What did you do the last 2 hours before you went to bed?					
What did you eat and/or drink the last 2 hours before bed?					

What time did you go to bed?					
How long did it take you to fall asleep?					
How many times did you wake up during the night?					
What thoughts were you having when you woke up?					
What did you do when you woke up during the night?					
Overall, how many hours did you sleep?					
Did you wake up earlier than you expected?					
What time did you get up for the day?					
On a scale of 1-5, did you feel groggy or rested when you woke?	1-groggy 2 3 4 5-rested				

Gary R. Plaford

On a scale of 1-5, did you feel fatigued or energetic during the day?	1-fatigued 2 3 4 5-energetic				
Did you take a nap, and if so, when and for how long?					

11. On a scale of 1-5, did you feel groggy or rested when you woke up? If you are consistently groggy when awakening this is an indication that you are consistently waking from deep sleep as opposed to REM sleep, and this is an indication that you are sleep deprived. That means you are either not getting enough sleep or you are not getting good quality sleep.

12. On a scale of 1-5, did you feel fatigued or energetic during the day? Again, this is an indication of the quality of sleep you are getting. If you are not getting quality sleep, that means you are lingering in stage two non-REM rather than getting enough deep sleep or REM sleep.

13. Did you take a nap, and if so when and for how long? Naps can be good for us or they can be bad for us (see the section on napping), but we can learn to us them effectively.

Keeping a sleep diary is an excellent way to pin down the issues we are having with sleep so that we can specifically address those issues. Besides the daily diary there are also some general questions that need to be answered.

Sleep Diary—General Questions

1. Generally how would you describe your sleep?

   _____

2. Do you have a normal bed time routine? If so, what is it?
   _____

3. Do you have a normal wake up routine, and if so what is that?
   _____

4. Do you sleep in total darkness?
   Explain._____

5. Do you sleep in quiet?
   Explain._____

6. What is the temperature set at when you sleep?
   _____

7. Do you experience sleep apnea or heavy snoring?
   Explain._____

8. Do you experience restless leg syndrome?
   How often/how severe? _____

9. Do you use alcohol, caffeine, or tobacco before bed?
   Explain._____

10. Do you ever nap? When, how often, and how long?
    _____

11. Do you exercise regularly?
    When and how much? _____

12. Do you meditate, practice deep breathing, or practice yoga
    or tai-chi?
    Explain. _____

13. Are your sleep problems: _____
    a. That you cannot get to sleep?
       _____

    b. That you wake up during the night?
       _____

    c. That you wake up early and cannot get back to sleep?
       _____

    d. That you are not getting good quality sleep?
       _____

e. That you sleep too much?

_____

f. That you do not feel rested after sleep?

_____

14. If you go to bed and do not immediately go to sleep, what do you do? _____

15. How late do you watch television or use your computer before bed? _____

16. Are there any other issues that disrupt or impact your sleep? Explain._____

In Summation

There are a number of physical strategies we can utilize to both lower and manage our stress more effectively. These include:

1. Exercise—The human body needs exercise. Some of us might get enough exercise, some might do aerobic exercise on a regular basis, but many of us don't. Exercise does not have to be aerobic to be beneficial. Walking thirty minutes a day, every day, will have a tremendous effect in our lives. After we feel comfortable with thirty minutes, increase it gradually to an hour. We can walk an hour at one time, or walk thirty minutes in the morning sunlight and another thirty minutes in the afternoon or evening. For those who do aerobic exercise, walk on the days you don't. Exercise will improve physical health, regulate metabolism, improve the immune response, regulate weight issues, improve cardiovascular health, improve mental functioning and mental outlook, as well as helping us to reduce and manage stress.

2. Yoga—Yoga relaxes the mind and body, and is a great tool to use as a de-stressor before bed.

3. Tai Chi—Tai Chi connects the mind and body and reduces stress like yoga, but also is a wonderful strategy to use as we age because it keeps the body moving gracefully and freely.

4. Deep breathing—Deep breathing focuses the mind on the physical act of breathing deeply into the abdomen, and it engages the parasympathetic nervous system which helps us slow down and de-stress.

5. Healthy lifestyle—This includes all of the above, but also means not using tobacco, monitoring the use of caffeine, controlling how and when we use alcohol, staying away from recreational drugs and prescription drugs that disrupt REM sleep, making sure we enjoy every day, planning for get-a-ways, and monitoring how much and when we watch television.

6. Diet—This means monitoring both the quantity and quality of the foods we use to fuel our bodies. Fast foods and snack foods should be used in moderation.

7. Sleep—This means taking the steps we need to take to improve the quality and quantity of both deep sleep and REM sleep. This would include using the senses, practicing good sleep hygiene, having bed time and wakeup time routines, not playing games with the snooze button, using light to regulate our sleep/wake schedule, improving sleep efficiency, using naps wisely, and utilizing a sleep diary.

CHAPTER 8

Mental Strategies for Managing Stress

There are events and there are moments that shape our lives. The events are the big things. They could include marriage, divorce, the death of a loved one, the birth of a child. These events often shape our lives in significant ways...positive or negative. There are also moments that shape our lives. A father taking his daughter to breakfast is a moment and not a very significant moment by itself. But if that father takes his daughter to breakfast every month, year after year, those moments become incredibly significant. Those moments build routines, traditions, relationships. We cannot always control the events in our lives, sometimes...sometimes not, they will happen. We can control moments...we can make those happen if we choose and plan to do so. Never underestimate the power of the moments we choose to make happen...moments we build brick by brick, drop by drop, moment by moment.

In any discussion about mental strategies for managing stress we must begin by keeping in mind the differences in the level of stress we are facing. As previously discussed, when we are facing mild to moderate stress we are more apt to look for ways to resolve or manage that stress. When we are in a high stress state we are near or in what we call "fight or flight" mode. In "fight or flight" we are not focused on resolving or managing the stress, we are focused on fleeing the stressed situation or protecting ourselves...fighting. Hence the term "fight or flight."

> In "fight or flight" we are not focused on resolving
>
> or managing stress, we are focused on fleeing the
>
> stressful situation or protecting ourselves.

High stress situations could include such things as being unemployed for an extended period of time and facing the prospect of losing your home and having no place to live for yourself and your children, or facing an upcoming retirement and fearing that there is not enough money saved to live on, or having a major illness or injury requiring extensive medical treatment with high medical bills and having no insurance to cover it, etc. These are high stress situations. These are situations that can cause us to be overwhelmed and result in "fight or flight" mode. We want to give up, we want to throw in the towel, we pack up our belongings and move to another city, we may become suicidal, or we do something else that is drastic.

There is nothing magical that we can do to reduce the stress from such situations. What we must do is face such situations and find some way to resolve the issues. Running from them or trying to find ways to avoid them will not resolve them. Only when we face such events or situations can we reduce the stress level from high to moderate, and only then can we utilize mental techniques to resolve/manage the stress even more. Sometimes facing a high stress, "fight or flight" situation involves nothing more than acceptance. Sometimes that is all we can do...accept the situation and the changes that the situation brings and then start over/again from there. There have been many people, for example, who have gone bankrupt...but bounced back. Before they bounced back, however, they had to accept the fact that they were in bankruptcy, that they had failed in some way, that there was nothing they could do in the situation they were in except end it...accept it...move on from there.

I hope I am not making this sound easy, because it isn't, but it can and has been done. The bottom line is this, there are situations we sometimes face in life that create high levels of stress. These high stress situations often put us in "fight or flight" mode. In "fight of flight" mode we are not looking to resolve or manage stress, we are looking to flee the stressful situation. Only when we lower the stress sufficiently to a moderate or mild level can we focus on implementing stress reduction or stress management techniques. Therefore, when we are in high stress situations we have to face whatever issues exist and resolve them to some extent. The resolution could be nothing more than accepting where we now are. Accepting where we are is a necessary part of planning what to do next. We cannot take the next step until we recognize and accept where we are.

If the stress isn't at the "fight or flight" level, or if we have reduced it from the "fight or flight" level, we can then focus more effectively on mental strategies. There are a number of mental strategies that we can utilize as a next step to resolve/manage stress. These would include such things as recognizing and avoiding stressors, addressing our mindset and perceptions, analyzing and reframing our assumptions, understanding and utilizing affirmations, addressing our problem solving and coping strategies, goal setting, boosting our self-confidence and self-esteem, using techniques that have been developed to reduce stress such as meditation, biofeedback, relaxation, and imagery, and scheduling time for ourselves. We will address each of these topics in turn.

Recognizing and avoiding stressors

The first step in recognizing stressors is to know what stresses us out. What causes that stress response in us? This includes the places that cause it, the people that cause it, and the situations that cause it. One typical place that causes stress is the work place. It can be that the job we do creates stress in us. If that is the case, then it might be wise to consider looking for a different job or at least planning for an early out from this job. If a specific job is creating stress for us on a consistent basis, then that job is taking a toll on our physical and mental health and happiness, and we must ask ourselves when enough is enough?.

On the other hand, it may not be the job itself that is causing stress but rather certain people with whom we work. We all have difficult people in our lives. Sometimes those are unfortunately relatives, but sometimes they are our fellow workers. One of the traits of difficult people is that they do not seem to recognize how they come across. Their level of emotional intelligence is such that they do not recognize what others are feeling, hence they do not and really cannot feel empathy for others. The recognition of emotions is the basis for empathy. Since difficult people cannot recognize what others are feeling they also cannot recognize what others are feeling about them, they cannot see how they are coming across. If they could see how others see them, in many cases these difficult people would change their behaviors. Since that is not the case, however, we get stuck dealing with them. If that person is a co-worker it can be difficult, but when that person is a supervisor it can really create problems for us and can generate high levels of stress.

Additionally, it may not be the job itself or necessarily the people we work with, but rather specific situations that we find stressful. Getting evaluated or evaluating someone we supervise may generate stress, or having to make a presentation to a group of potential clients, or completing the paper work requirements for the job may generate stress. In other words it may be certain parts of the job or certain tasks associated with the job that are the stressors.

If we can determine that the stress we are having is work related, then there are steps we can take to alleviate or manage that stress better. First of all, evaluate the job. Look at the formal

Gary R. Plaford

job description. What are we being asked to do? What are the expectations? Can we comfortably meet all of these expectations, or do we need some additional training to address some area where we might be weak? We may be good at a job except for one or two elements, and we cover our deficits by focusing on what we do best. However, it may be those one or two deficits that are generating most of our stress. When that is the case, find out what training, what advice, what assistance we can get to better our understanding and performance in those areas. Doing that will reduce the stress. For example, if we are good at our job but occasionally we must speak publicly and we are stressed about that, then we can get involved with groups like "Toastmasters International," a non-profit organization, where we can learn and practice speaking in front of others.

Besides evaluating our job it is a good idea to understand the priorities of our boss or direct supervisor. What are they looking for? What do they see as the keys to the job? What is most important to them? This can vary by supervisor. Some supervisors want every "i" dotted and every "t" crossed in the paperwork. For others the paperwork may be secondary. If we are used to performing in one way for a certain supervisor, and through promotion or attrition that supervisor changes, we need to find out what this new supervisor expects rather than merely assuming everything will be the same. When there are inconsistencies regarding how things are done or viewed, it is best to work these out early. This will avoid a lot of future stress.

Additionally it is always wise to look at the climate and culture or the work place. Climate is defined in terms of employees' perceptions of their work environment. The climate for an individual is that individual's perception of the psychological impact of the work environment on his/her personal well-being. An organizational climate is where employees share these same or similar perceptions.

Culture, on the other hand, refers to the norms and beliefs of the work place. This includes shared values, shared beliefs, and shared behavioral norms. Shared values refer to the shared views or attitudes about what is really valued, what is important, what is prized here. Different values exist in different organizations. In some getting to work on time is valued, in others it may be staying late to get the job done, or being non-confrontational and supportive, or making sure every view point is expressed. The values shared in different organizations, even similar organizations that espouse to have similar goals, can be greatly different. Shared beliefs are also a part of the culture. Beliefs refer to shared convictions that certain things are true. Beliefs are not easily changed by rational argument. For example, many Americans believe that women have the right to opt for abortion, while many other Americans believe the opposite. There are organizations that share similar beliefs about this...one way or the other. Likewise, there are certain shared beliefs about education held by educational groups, but the shared beliefs of some charter school groups or some political groups may be somewhat different. This third component of culture is the shared behavioral norms. These are based on the shared values and beliefs, which become the guides to conduct, standards, and rules.

These aspects of climate and culture influence how an organization functions, and how individual members of that organization function. Climate and culture define boundaries for us within an organization. They convey a sense of identity within an organization. They facilitate a commitment to a larger purpose or greater good, they give us purpose. They maintain social stability...they provide the glue that holds the organization together. And they serve as a control mechanism that guides and shapes the attitudes and behaviors of both new and continued employees.

Having said that, it is important to understand that if the climate and culture are out of sync in an organization or we are out of sync with what exists in an organization, this can create stress. The climate and culture can become out of sync because of changes in staffing or management, or because of new directives from the main office, or because of changes in government regulations that affect how an organizations functions. Individuals can get out of sync with an organization because they cannot go along with changes that occur, or they develop new beliefs or values. If it is the climate or culture of an organization that is the cause of our stress, then that is what we need to address. We may need to take a close, hard look at what we believe and what we value and determine if these are in sync with the organization. Ethical dilemmas fall in this category. In fact the entire organization could be out of sync because of new management. If this is the case, what can we do to get people on the same page, so to speak? If we cannot determine a way to either fit in with the culture or change the culture, then it is time to make an exit plan. Just living with the stress, if it is high stress, should not be an option. That becomes very unhealthy physically and mentally both for us and for those around us.

Once we have evaluated the job, examined the expectations our boss and others have for us, and examined the climate and culture of an organization, it is important to take action. Learn what we need to learn. Update skills or knowledge in certain areas if necessary. Drop the less important tasks and focus our resources on the tasks that our boss and the organization value most, create a "stop doing" list...stop wasting time on things that are interfering with more important functions. Also, stop fighting battles that don't need to be fought. In other words we need to pick our battles more wisely. There comes a time when we all must realize we cannot fight every battle that comes along. None of us has that energy, and trying to do so generates an incredible amount of stress in our lives.

While the work place can be and often is a place that generates stress, so can the home. Living with others means compromise, we don't get everything we want when we want it. Raising children can tax our patience to the max. These conflicts and stresses are more often generated by relationship issues. This is where an understanding of emotional intelligence becomes important. In chapter two we discussed emotional intelligence. The domains of emotional intelligence include the recognition of emotions and one's own emotions, managing one's emotions, motivating one-self and delaying gratification, recognizing emotions in others and feeling empathy for others, and establishing and managing relationships with others over time. Relationship issues concern the last two of these domains, but having the last two domains is dependent on the development of the first three. We cannot recognize emotions in others and feel empathy for others unless we can recognize emotions in ourselves. We cannot maintain long term relationships unless we can feel empathy for the other person and respond appropriately to their needs, and we cannot respond appropriately to their needs unless we can manage our own emotions and delay our own gratification.

With this in mind, the first step in regard to emotional intelligence is to evaluate your own level of emotional intelligence. Do we recognize what we are feeling when we are feeling it, or do we fly into rages and later feel regretful? Do we recognize when emotions are building up in us before they become uncontrollable, or can we soothe ourselves and calm ourselves down? What strategies do we have for doing so? Do we need to develop additional strategies? Are we impulsive and need to have our way or need to have what we want now, or can we stifle impulses and delay gratification? Again, do we have strategies to accomplish this or do we need to establish some strategies to broaden our ability to delay gratification? Do we recognize emotions in others and do we often feel empathy for others or find it easy to feel empathy for others? Can we tell what other people think about us? The recognition of what others are feeling is the ultimate people skill because the ability to feel empathy is based on that. Finally, can we maintain relationships over a long period of time or are we in and out of relationships like a revolving door? The ability to maintain relationships means that we can feel empathy for the other person and respond appropriately to their needs. This is the basis for sharing, for taking turns, for really listening to the other person rather than merely waiting our own turn to talk.

If we see that we have problems in any of these areas, then these are things we need to address because these problems will generate stress in our lives. There are things that can be done to address these issues. Playing emotional charades, acting out emotions, discussing the emotions that actors have in movies, these are all techniques for improving the recognition of emotions. Managing emotions and delaying gratification can often be improved by developing routines. Routines are habitual ways of both thinking and acting to address our emotional responses. These will be discussed further in the next chapter. A great way to develop empathy is to listen, really listen, to the other person; your wife, your husband, your child. Really listen. Don't judge and don't jump in with advice. We need to try to ask ourselves how we would feel if we were in this predicament. Another way to address empathy is to put ourselves out there. Volunteer to help others; the elderly, the needy, children, cats and dogs. Putting ourselves in a position to see needs is a great technique for learning to see needs.

Tips for Parents and Educators

Historically emotional intelligence has been passed to our children by modeling it. In our fast paced society, however, the amount of time parents spend with children has dramatically gone down. This is because of technology as well as the hectic schedules that everyone has. The point is, since less actual time is spent with our children, there is less time to model emotional intelligence. The solution to this, other than actually spending more time with our children, is to not only model emotional intelligence but to specifically teach it. How do we do that? We begin by discussing emotions with our children. At home, when we watch a movie with them, talk about the emotions of the characters. Even cartoon characters display emotions.

Ask the child what the character was feeling, why do you think he was feeling that, what was he doing that made you think he was feeling that, what would you have felt in the same situation? This helps them recognize emotions, relate to the character, and begin to feel empathy for the character. Likewise, in schools we have students read and write about stories. Why not ask them to write about the emotions the characters were experiencing? They are still reading and writing, which is the educational goal, but we can further their emotional intelligence by having them identify, discuss, and relate to those emotions.

We practice the piano, we practice multiplication tables, we practice our spelling words, we practice shooting free throws with a basketball, yet we leave the development of emotional intelligence to chance. This is a huge mistake, and one we do not have to continue to make. Emotional intelligence, the ability to manage our emotions and delay gratification, underlies all achievement. The ability to recognize emotions in ourselves and others is the basis for establishing and maintaining relationships with others. These are critical aspects of living a happy and successful life.

A strategy that works in all of these areas is to work on relationships, to build relationships. What does this mean? For example, there are events and there are moments in our lives. I referred to that in the opening thought for this chapter. The events are the big things that happen in life. We control some of these events by the choices we make and the actions we take, but some of the big events in our lives come about regardless of what we choose or what we do. We cannot control the death of a loved one, or the decision of a spouse who wants a divorce, or the decisions or actions of our children. Our control over events is limited. The moments in our lives, however, are the little things. These are the things we decide to do, or the things we decide not to do, on a regular basis. Taking a son or daughter to breakfast once a week or once a month, just the two of you, year after year is a great example. Each and every occasion in itself is merely a moment, but such moments, repeated routinely, become incredibly special. These special moments build relationships. Taking the time, making the effort to build such relationships by creating such moments pays off especially when stress enters the picture.

The final topic I want to address in recognizing and avoiding stressors is to recognize what we can control and what we cannot control in life. There are things in life that we can control and there are things that we cannot control. Unfortunately, what we often do is to focus on those things that we cannot control. We worry and fret about them. All of our attention and energy is devoted to them...and we end up in a state of high stress over them. While we are focusing all of our attention on these issues that we really cannot control, we are ignoring the things that we could control. Now those issues also stress us because we have not addressed them. Whenever we are stressed it is of utmost importance to evaluate what aspects of the issue we can and cannot control. The things that are out of our control must not be the center of our endeavors. Instead we need to really focus all of our efforts on those things that are in our control. It is easier in the short term just to worry, but it is better and less stressful for us in the long term to evaluate what we really can control, and then focus on those things.

Addressing Mindset and Perception

A second mental strategy for managing stress is to assess and address mindset. As discussed in chapter five, mindset is how we see ourselves and our abilities. Do we believe our abilities are set, or do we believe that we can improve our abilities and rise to occasions? When we are faced with a challenge of any kind, if we do not believe we can successfully meet that challenge, then our stress level goes up dramatically. We may try to avoid the challenge, run from the challenge, or bring up other issues to muddy the water in an attempt to protect ourselves from failure. If we believe that we cannot meet a specific challenge and will never be capable of meeting that challenge, that will have a significant impact on what we are willing to attempt and what we are willing to risk. On the other hand, if we believe that although we cannot meet a challenge now but with some effort would be able to meet that challenge successfully, that will lead to different choices and affect our stress in a different manner.

What is important is to understand how the brain works and how learning occurs. As we learn any task, as we do something over and over, the brain forges neural pathways. The brain changes. It does not stay the same. Likewise, our abilities do not stay the same. As the brain changes in regard to specific tasks, our ability to deal with those tasks also changes. We grow. As we practice any task we get better at it. This is true of anything we do, of anything we put our mind to. Certainly there are things that at any given point we cannot do or cannot do well, but if we have the determination to try those things over and over we will get better at doing them. If we can know that deep down, that will lower our stress when we face difficult tasks.

This may sound simple to someone who has a growth mindset, but for someone who does not have such a mindset, this is a significant change in the way we look at things. It is critical to train ourselves to look at things form this growth mindset. If we truly believe we can accomplish anything over time if we choose to make the effort, that will significantly lower stress. We may not choose to accomplish certain things, but knowing that we could do so is important. I used to play the piano. I know that if I chose to take lessons, even at my age, I could learn to do so again. It is my choice. Likewise, some adults and some children do not read. If they believe they cannot learn to read, then they will avoid reading at all costs. They will find excuses not to try. This is an embarrassment and a stressor for them. Often they will give up on reading because of this stress, it counts less as a failure if we failed because we didn't try than if we failed because we couldn't do it. On the other hand, knowing, really knowing that we can do it if we try is a huge stress relief. Most people who do not read are capable of reading if they truly put forth the effort. It may take a little longer for some than for others, but it is an achievable task for most of us. If we can teach people this, if we can train ourselves to have this mindset, we can significantly impact the stress in our lives.

The issue of mindset also comes into play when we look at such things as cognitive overload. This occurs when we have too much information coming in too quickly and we get to the point where we cannot deal with it. We are overwhelmed. Under such circumstances we must consider the speed of the information coming at us, the interruptions, and the introduction of other aspects of the issue before we have successfully integrated the previous aspects... hence the sensation of being overwhelmed. It is important to give ourselves time to think, to limit the interruptions, and to focus on one issue at a time. Doing that can help us realize that we really can cope with it, we just need the time to do so.

The same thing can occur from multitasking. We form the illusion that we are addressing multiple issues at once when in reality we are addressing multiple issues poorly at once. Then we become overwhelmed because we have not accomplished a great deal and things are backing up on us. Again, what is important is to make the effort to look at one item at a time. This will put us back in control and lower the stress.

Analyzing and Reframing Assumptions

Besides mindset, it is critical to evaluate the assumptions we make. We often think in terms of people being optimists or pessimists. In reality, these are habitual forms of thinking. Just like we have behavioral habits, we have thought habits. Optimists and pessimists have different habits in the way they think. For example, when something bad happens an optimist will think about the bad event, while a pessimist will think of it in terms of permanence. An optimist might say, "I failed at that task today." A pessimist might say, "I failed again." There is more of a permanence about the failure with the pessimist. Additionally there is more pervasiveness. While the optimist might say, "I failed," the pessimist might say, "I am a failure." Finally, with the pessimist there is more personalization. The pessimist finds someone to blame, even if that person is himself. The optimist is less quick at finding fault with himself or someone else, but rather looks at why the events occurred as they did, "Maybe I was not as prepared as I should have been. If I'm more prepared next time this won't happen."

The point is, this thinking is habitual, and it is learned. The good news is, we can learn to think differently...we can develop different thought habits. But to do so, we must first understand the thought habits we have. It is very helpful to keep a diary for several days noting such situations. What are the thoughts we are having? Is there permanence to the way we think, do we think in terms like always or never? Is there pervasiveness to the way we think, are we over-generalizing events? Are we personalizing events and blaming either ourselves or others, or are we looking more at solutions than at whose fault it is? When we think in these pessimistic ways we set ourselves up for stress. These pessimistic tendencies are the basis for the assumptions we make. Understanding how we think is the first step in changing how we think.

Take the Optimist vs. Pessimist Quiz. Look over your responses. Generally responses "a, b, and c" to the quiz reflect the permanence, pervasiveness, and personalization of pessimistic thinking. The "d" answer generally reflects a more optimistic outlook. The answers you give are a measure, and merely a measure, of whether your thinking is generally pessimistic or optimistic, and whether or not these thought habits are something you need to address.

Optimist vs. Pessimist Quiz

1. When something goes wrong, you think...?
   a. I knew something bad was going to happen...things were too good to last.
   b. What else will go wrong...trouble always comes in bunches?
   c. Who caused this? Did I do something wrong?
   d. Things will work out if I just hang in there.
2. If you get a message that your boyfriend/girlfriend needs to see you tonight because they have something important to say, you think....?
   a. They have a problem they need to talk to me about.
   b. They are breaking up with me.
   c. They are unhappy with me about something.
   d. They have something important to say...I can't wait to hear what it is.
3. When you consider success, you think...?
   a. Success is mostly about luck, fate, and chance.
   b. Enjoy it while it lasts because failure is just around the corner.
   c. Other people will keep you from being successful if they have the chance.
   d. With hard work I can accomplish anything.
4. You have a fight with your boyfriend/girlfriend, you think...?
   a. Our relationship is over.
   b. If he/she doesn't apologize our relationship is over.
   c. This is all his/her fault.
   d. If we talk this out we'll get through it.
5. Picturing yourself in ten years, you think...?
   a. I probably won't be here.
   b. It will be harrier and scarier.
   c. It depends on what other people in my life do.
   d. Things will be better...they always get better.
6. Considering your own typical outlook, you think...?
   a. Don't try to do too much...that always leads to failure.
   b. Some things are just not going to work our regardless of how hard I try.
   c. Whenever things go wrong there is always someone to blame.
   d. Nothing is impossible if I put my mind to it.
7. You wake up late for work and you think...?
   a. I'm in big trouble...I might get fired.
   b. I'm so stupid for letting this happen.
   c. I'll call in and tell them I'm sick and was too ill to call in earlier.
   d. I'll call and tell them I overslept and will be in shortly.
8. When considering the topic of effort, you think...?
   a. Don't try something unless I know I will be successful.
   b. If I try and fail I am a failure...so why try?
   c. If I was really smart I wouldn't have to work so hard.
   d. Effort is a good thing. It leads to success.

Affirmations

The second step in changing how we think is to change our assumptions. This is where affirmations come in. We use affirmations all the time, whether we realize it or not. Affirmations can be positive or negative. Although we typically think of affirmations as positive, they can also be negative. To "affirm" means "to declare firmly, to maintain to be true, to uphold, or to confirm." Hence, what we declare firmly to be true, uphold, or confirm can be negative in nature as well as positive. Affirmations are the little messages we give ourselves, positive or negative, over and over every day. The point is, we respond to these messages. They are our reality. The truth about reality is that there is no one reality out there. I respond to what I perceive is out there. I respond to what I believe, to what I see, and to how I interpret the events that happen in my life. This may be in some ways different and in some ways similar to how you might respond to the same events, but I can only respond to what I perceive is reality. It is not the events that occur in my life that I respond to, it is my interpretation of the events that shape my responses. The affirmations we utilize, positive or negative, are what determine how we interpret life events. In other words, our affirmations shape our reality.

We see this over and over in life. Most of us experience the death of a loved one, but how we deal with it is determined by how we interpret it. If we tell ourselves over and over that this is horrible, that this is unfair, that we cannot live with this, that is when we need to watch out for potential suicide. If, on the other hand, we tell ourselves that although this is horrible we can get through it, we can go on, we can and must continue to live life for ourselves and for the other significant people in our lives, then we grieve the death but eventually begin to live life again. It is not the event but the interpretation of the event that determines our response.

During the Korean conflict it was noted that many of our soldiers who became prisoners of war died in confinement. There were other allied forces that had much lower mortality rates as prisoners of war. Why was that? It was discovered that training was critical, that teaching soldiers how to think about, how to interpret, how to evaluate their capture and confinement was a critical aspect of mortality rates. This ultimately impacted how we trained soldiers.

When we think about road rage, what do we see? Does road rage just suddenly occur out of the blue? No, it does not. Road rage develops over time. Road rage develops because of the continual, repeated messages we give ourselves about other drivers, their driving abilities, the danger they present, etc. We allow ourselves to have and repeat these negative messages over and over again, and eventually it manifests itself as road rage. If we are effectively going to address road rage we cannot merely look at the individual's behavior, the road rage itself, but rather at the habitual thoughts they had that got them to this point. Those negative affirmations are what we must address and change. The most effective way to change them is not to try to ignore them, to not give into them, but rather to replace them with more positive affirmations.

Whenever we are dealing with habitual behavior, whether it is actual behavior or thought patterns, the key is not to try not to do something, but rather to replace that behavior or that thought with more positive, more appropriate thoughts. Habits are difficult to change. They will always be difficult to change. The most effective strategy is not to try to change them but rather to replace them with more appropriate habits...including thought habits. This is what using positive affirmations is all about.

It is also important to note that using affirmations effectively takes time, commitment, and consistency. I remember visiting the Grand Canyon, and what a magnificent sight that is. At the bottom of this awesome, world wonder flows the Colorado River. But the Colorado River doesn't merely flow though the bottom of this spectacular canyon, it made this canyon. But it didn't make this canyon overnight, it took centuries to achieve. It took time and consistency. Likewise, using positive affirmations to change the way we think about something takes time, commitment, and consistency... although hopefully not centuries. We're talking about replacing habits with different habits, replacing thoughts with different thoughts. If we are willing to make that commitment we will eventually reap the benefits. Positive affirmations can change the way we think, which means they can change our perception of reality, which means they can change the responses we have to events in our lives.

The most effective affirmations come from looking at the negative thoughts we have related to specific events, and replacing those negative thoughts with positive affirmations. In chapter six we discussed the nine automatic negative thoughts Dr. Amen describes so well. Let's revisit those. The first was "All or nothing thinking." If we think in terms like this, that everything is good or bad, black or white, positive or negative, then we need to challenge those thoughts. They need to be replaced with the idea that things can be both good and bad, that there can be positive and negative in the same event, and that what is important is what we choose to focus on, the good or the evil that is present.

The second automatic negative thought is "Always thinking." If we think in terms like always, never, no one, everyone, all the time, etc., that generates stress. In truth we aren't always last, it isn't that we never get our turn. It may feel like it sometimes, but that is not the case. If we think like that we need to challenge those thoughts and replace them with the reality that we do get our turn, and will get our turn, and we need to appreciate it when our turn comes.

"Focusing on the negative" is the third type of automatic thought that gets in our way. If we choose to have this focus then we miss all the good things that happen in life. There is good and bad in everything if we look for it, and if we always look for the negative we can always find it. We need to replace focusing on the negative with focusing on the positive. This is not a Pollyanna approach. The focus we have determines the behaviors we choose to employ.

"Fortunetelling" is the fourth automatic negative thought. If our habit is to predict that we will fail, then more often than not

Gary R. Plaford

we will fail. The prediction itself influences the outcome. We need to replace that thought habit with thoughts such as, "when I do my best I have succeeded," or "when I truly make the effort I improve my skills and abilities and I get better at the task," or "if I get up one more time than I fall down I will eventually be successful."

The fifth automatic negative thought is "Mind reading." If we habitually think that others are thinking bad things about us, that has an impact on how we behave as well as on our self-esteem. The truth is we usually do not know what others are thinking and even if we did it is a waste of time going there. If we habitually think like this we need to replace it with the idea that we will do our best and then whatever happens, happens. If they like me great, if they don't, I cannot control that.

The sixth automatic negative thought is "Thinking with our feelings." Our feelings, our emotions help us think and help us decide. They are tools in our arsenal for decision making. However, emotions are tricky and can lead us down a slippery slope if we merely accept them without question. For example, we make a mistake and feel embarrassed and incompetent, so we tell ourselves we are stupid. "I'm stupid, stupid, stupid." Chances are we are not really stupid, but rather we weren't focused, we weren't paying attention to what we were doing, our mind was elsewhere, we let habit take over instead of thinking our way through something, and it ended up wrong. We need to stop doing that to ourselves and rather evaluate what really happened. The message needs to be, "I'm not stupid, but I need to pay closer attention to what I'm doing." "I am capable, I just need to focus."

"Guilt beatings" is the seventh automatic negative thought. When we lay on the guilt by habitually telling ourselves we should do this, we ought to do that, we must act accordingly, we are setting ourselves up for guilt and stress. We need to stop such habits and decide how to act based on what is right and wrong, what is moral and immoral, not because we feel guilt or shame.

The eighth automatic negative thought is "Labeling." When we habitually label ourselves because of actions or events, those labels begin to impact our expectations and our behaviors. The labels we give ourselves can be positive or negative. When they are negative we need to replace them with positives.

Finally, the last automatic negative thought is "Blame." When we habitually find someone or something to blame when things go wrong, we never end up taking responsibility for the situation. If we don't take responsibility then we can never control or manage the situation. The first step in controlling one's own behavior is to own the behavior. If we don't own it we can never control it. We need to get out of the habit of blaming others or blaming circumstances when things go wrong. We need to own up to our part in the fiasco. Then, and only then, can we look at what we need to do to make sure this doesn't happen again. "I am responsible for my actions," is a good affirmation.

Social Commentary

One of the issues we face today is that of the growing litigious nature of our society. We sue each other at the drop of a hat. We are trying to find blame in every situation. In reality, there is not someone or something to blame in every situation. Sometimes things just happen, and sometimes it is our own lack of focus that causes things to happen. Always blaming someone else is socially and morally a dangerous and slippery slope for a society.

In the previous section we discussed analyzing the negative assumptions we make. Those negative assumptions, in addition to the automatic negative thoughts just discussed, are key in creating the positive affirmations we want. Some examples of positive affirmations are included in the following text box.

Positive Affirmation Examples

I can overcome this obstacle.

I can let this issue go.

I can feel the stress leaving my body.

I deserve to be happy.

I have the power to change things in my life.

I can forgive others.

When I have done my best, that is all I can do, and it is enough.

I can choose to be happy regardless of the circumstances.

I can choose to be happy regardless of what others think.

I can be flexible and open to change.

I am worthy of happiness.

Problem Solving

Another mental strategy for coping with and/or eliminating stress is to foster good problem solving skills. Problem solving is a learned skill. When we don't have good problems solving skills, and something goes wrong in our world, we are more apt to fall apart, to not handle it well, to succumb to the stress generated, to often create more stress by handling the situation poorly, etc.

When we do have good problem solving skills we are not enslaved by the emotions of the situation. We are not destined to merely react to the situation, but we can evaluate the situation from various perspectives and determine what actions on our part will most likely alleviate the problem and the stress. This is the difference between falling apart, flying into a rage, or making the rational decisions that will most benefit us.

So what are the steps of effective problem solving? The first step is to realize that we have a problem solving strategy and to take a step back to allow ourselves to engage that strategy. This means not flying into a rage or falling to pieces, but rather reminding ourselves that we have specific steps that we must now take.

The second step is to make the effort to determine what the problem really is. Sometimes this is very easy, but sometimes it can be extremely complex. Too often we are swayed by our biases, our friendships, or our affiliations and we make sweeping generalizations that further confuse the matter. It is important here to be honest with ourselves about what the issue really is if we are going to effectively address it, otherwise we are just wasting our time.

The third step in problem solving is to brainstorm what options we have. We are not at the point of making a decision here; we are merely looking at all the possible options we have. In doing so it is important to include all of the possible actions we could take, regardless of how lame or idiotic some of them may seem. Get all of the options down on paper, the seemingly good options and the seemingly poor options. This becomes the basis for the ultimate choices we make.

The next step is to determine what outcome we want. What would we really like to happen at this point? Given what has occurred, what would we like to happen now? What is the best scenario available? The question, "What do I really want?" is a significant question to ask.

The next step is to look at all of the options we wrote down while brainstorming and determine which of these is most likely to get us what we want? What we may want, for example, is to keep our job. What we may like to do is slap someone in the face. But will slapping that person in the face be the best option for keeping our job, or will another course of action more likely achieve that end? If we are sure what we really want, then what action on our part is most likely to get us there?

The final step is to implement that action. If we are unsuccessful then we need to restart the process, but what we have achieved is handling the situation in a saner, more rational manner rather than letting emotions dictate our responses. In the long run, even if this does not pay dividends in a given situation, it will reduce our stress and make us more likely to be successful in meeting our needs.

This is a rational approach to problem solving and decision making, but it is not the only approach people use. Some people do not problem solve at all but merely react to situations emotionally. This approach results in outbursts of anger and sorrow, aggression, and moodiness. There are also many people who use a behavioral model of decision making and problem solving. This is where they identify a problem, identify a possible solution, and try it. If it does not work, then try to identify another solution. They are basically not looking for the best solution, but for anything that will work. This may save a little time in the short term, but long term it causes more issues. This results in constantly revisiting the same issues over and over again. The adage "if it is worth doing it is worth doing well," is appropriate here.

Another strategy for problem solving and decision making is referred to as the garbage can model. This is basically where we have a mix of typical problems we face and a mix of typical solutions, and when a problem arises we throw our favorite solutions at it and hope it works. This is not really an effective means of problem solving but it is one we often see from politicians and political parties. They don't' really make the effort to solve problems but rather throw solutions at them and hope something sticks.

The bottom line is we all face problems on a regular basis. Having the skills to solve problems when they arise is critical to managing, reducing, or even eliminating some of the stress in our lives. The alternative is to be led by our emotions in reacting to problems, and then ultimately having to face the added problems that emerge as a result of our initial reactions.

Goal Setting

Yet another mental strategy for dealing with stress is that of goal setting and planning. Goal setting, like some of the other issues already discussed, is in some ways a multi-categorical issue. In other words, it falls not only under the category of mental strategies for managing stress but also under spiritual and even emotional strategies. Hence, while certain aspects of goal setting will be discussed here, it will also be discussed, in a slightly different context, when we come to spiritual strategies. For now, however, it is important to look at the fact that we do have goals. So, what are our goals? We all have multiple issues and interests in our lives, but the importance of these issues varies greatly. Some things are much more important to us than others. Yet how often do we really consider what it is that we really value? How often do we look at the goals we have and consciously realize that these issues are more important to us than those issues?

Lots of issues in life can stress us out, but the only ones that we really should be concerned over are the ones that are truly important to us. Why should we allow ourselves to become stressed over issues that we really find secondary in the scheme of things? Yet if we don't do some goal setting, how do we determine which issues are primary and which are secondary?

The goals we have may be health and wellness goals. They may be educational goals. They may be achievement goals. They may be family or relationship goals. They might be financial or security goals. They might be balance goals; finding the right combination between work, family, and leisure. They might be travel goals. They could be community or philanthropic goals. They could be personal goals of some kind, or there might be other goals not covered in the above list. Whatever our goals are, or whatever combination of goals we have, we need to consciously evaluate them. Knowing what is important to us, having this in our consciousness, can help us not get too stressed over issues and events that fall outside of these areas.

There are multiple goal setting programs that can be utilized to evaluate our goals, but simply they should have us look at the goals we might have in different categories, rank these goals in order of importance, and then evaluate what we are doing in life and align our actions with what we have determined is really important to us. The attached chart (following page) can be used as a start in accomplishing this. Write down the goals you have in each category. This does not mean you have goals in each category; you may or may not, but write down the goals that you do have. After that go back and rank order these goals. Put "# 1" by the goal that is truly the most important to you. Put "# 2" by the second most important goal. Be honest here. Don't rank the goals by what you think they should be, but what they really are to you. After you have evaluated your list and ranked them as honestly as you can, look over the list and determine if the way you spend your time every day is in accordance with what your goals really are. If they are not, this is probably one of the causes of the stress you are facing. When our actions and behaviors are not in line with the goals we have this becomes an avenue for anxiety, unhappiness, and stress.

Self-Confidence / Self-Esteem

Another mental strategy for managing stress is to evaluate and build the level of self-confidence and self-esteem that we have. Self-confidence and self-esteem are not constants. They ebb and flow depending on the situations we are in. We have more confidence facing certain issues that we do when facing other issues. Even with issues where we have most confidence, sometimes we feel more confident and assured than at other times.

When we find ourselves in situations where our confidence is low, or has diminished, that is when we begin to feel the stress. That is when we are most likely to succumb to the pressure and the stress and not do our best. When we go into situations assured that we can handle it, that we can manage whatever comes at us, that is when we truly are at our best. That is when the stress is diminished and when we can best handle whatever stress exists.

Goals

(Write down your top one or two goals under each category)

Health and Wellness:
1.
2.
Education:
1.
2.
Achievement/Work:
1.
2.
Family/Relationships:
1.
2.
Financial/Security:
1.
2.
Balance between Work, Family, and Leisure:
1.
2.
Community/Philanthropic:
1.
2.
Travel/Adventure:
1.
2.
Personal/Other:
1.

2.

Gary R. Plaford

What are the signs of self-confidence or a lack of self-confidence? Do we do what is right even if it goes against the majority, or is our behavior and our action based on what other people think or what we think they think? Are we willing to take risks and put in the effort to accomplish something, or do we stay in our comfort zone to avoid the possibility of failure? Do we admit our mistakes, own up to them, and try to learn from them, or do we try to cover up our mistakes, blame others for our failures, or hide mistakes hoping no one will pin it on us? Can we wait for others to notice our accomplishments if and when they do, or do we brag, blow our own horn, or criticize others so we look better by comparison? Do we accept compliments graciously and recognize that our achievements came from effort and hard work, or do we dismiss compliments because we feel unworthy or because we feel it was really just luck or chance?

Recognizing whether or not we have self-confidence is one thing, but building it is another. So how do we go about building self-confidence and self-esteem? Let's begin with self-confidence. Having self-confidence in a given situation means that we believe in our ability to deal with, manage, or succeed in that given situation or at that given task. Albert Bandura describes this as self-efficacy. In his book *Self-Efficacy: The Exercise of Control*, Bandura describes four sources for self-efficacy. These include mastery experiences, vicarious experiences, social persuasion, and emotional status. Mastery experiences refer to those things that we have succeeded at, our actual successes. Vicarious experiences refer to seeing people similar to us succeed. The idea we come away with is "if he can do it then I can do it." Social persuasion refers to what others tell us. This includes the pat on the back, the encouragement, the belief they put in us, the pep talks. Emotional status refers to the idea that we have to manage our stress and remain positive. It is the idea that I really can do it if I just keep working at it.

How can we put these ideas into practice? We can address mastery experiences by looking at the successes we have already had, and by setting up experiences that we can be successful at. This involves practice and effort. We can address vicarious experiences by looking at others who have been successful as an example. They become our guides, our heroes. How did they achieve it? What did they do? How hard did they work? We can address social persuasion by putting ourselves around the right people. We cannot choose our families, but we can choose our friends. We can choose who we hang with. If we choose to be around positive people, people who have the same ideals and goals that we have, we are much more likely to receive the support and recognition we need. Finally, we can address emotional status by addressing our mindset, learning to be optimistic and positive, and managing our stress.

When I think about self-confidence I like to begin with some ideas fostered by Dr. William Hollowell, a well known child psychiatrist. He talks about what it takes in childhood to become a happy and productive member of the adult world. He states that there are five key things that must happen. The first is that the child must experience a sense of connection. There must be adults, or at least one adult, that the child feels accepts them as they are. This connection, this love, this acceptance is unconditional. It is not based on achievement or behavior, on what the child does or how the child acts. This does not mean there is not supervision, expectations, or discipline meted out by the adult, but that the connection is unconditional.

The second necessity Hollowell discusses is that there must be play. It is through play that we discover our world as well as discovering what it is we like and enjoy. This is when we are at one with a task, this is when we have maximum focus and concentration. Play is critical in finding out what it is that turns us on. It begins to give us direction in life, and motivation toward those interests. Play involves using our imagination and creativity; it is not about playing video games or watching television. We imagine and play at being a fireman, or a doctor, or a policeman, or whatever, and this starts us down the road to making choices about what we will eventually do with our lives. We begin to rule things in and rule things out through play. Play is critical because this is where motivation begins.

The third necessity is practice. Once we find what it is we love to do, we will practice that. When a child learns that he loves basketball he will go practice basketball, he doesn't have to be told to practice. We may guide a child and help them know how to practice or what to practice, but when a child finds something that they truly love they will practice. This is the beginning of discipline, of delaying gratification, of stifling impulses to achieve a goal.

The fourth necessity Hollowell cites is that of mastery. This means we get better at a task as we practice that task. It does not mean that we are necessarily the best at the task, but that we are better today than we were yesterday. This comes with the recognition that we will also be better tomorrow than we are today. This is the beginning of self-efficacy, of self-esteem, of self-confidence. The effort we are making is paying dividends, and we can see it.

Finally, there is recognition from others. Others notice the work we are putting in and that we are getting better at whatever task it is, and they recognize us for that effort. Notice, this is recognition for effort not for intelligence. This recognition may come as an official award, or a comment in front of the group, or merely a nod of approval, but it builds a connection to the larger group. This growing connection to the larger group is the basis for moral behavior. We do not harm, damage, steal from, disrespect, dis, or rebel from a group that we truly have a connection with. When adolescents rebel from authority or rebel against their parents, what we typically see is a lack of connection. I'm not talking about misbehavior; I'm talking about rejecting standards and ideals. When strong connections exist, it is those connections that create and enforce appropriate behavior in and toward the larger group.

Hollowell's 5 Keys to Adult Happiness

Connections...unconditional love

Play...the basis for motivation

Practice...the foundation of discipline

Mastery...the beginning of self esteem

Recognition...the foundation for moral behavior

Hollowell's five keys in becoming a happy and productive adult; connections, play, practice, mastery, and recognition provide a blue print for attaining self-confidence. Having positive connections provides the foundation and opportunity for both modeling behaviors and support. As adults we don't need play in the same way that children do, but we need the same result. For children play is the beginning of giving us direction in life. As adults we need to determine what direction we are going in life, what is important to us. Then we can begin to be more rational and direct about what we want and need. The direction is necessary in helping us to make those determinations. Practice is still critical. Once we decide what we want then we need to practice those skills that will get us there. Mastery is also critical. We need to recognize that we are mastering certain tasks, that we are getting better, that the practice and effort we have put in is paying off. Finally comes recognition. We need to recognize that we have achieved or are achieving something of value, but it sure helps when others that we care about notice it too.

Self-confidence and self-esteem are often used almost interchangeably, but there is a difference. Self-confidence refers to how we see our ability to handle or cope with specific situations. Self-esteem is a more general feeling we have toward ourselves, an overall appraisal of our self-worth. It involves being happy with or contented with ourselves and our abilities. Basically, however, if we work on building our self-confidence then we should have an improved sense of self-esteem.

Meditation, Bio-feedback, Relaxation, Imagery

Another mental strategy for managing stress is to learn one of the various techniques that have been developed to deal with stress. We have already discussed yoga, Tai-chi, and deep breathing as techniques under physical strategies. Strategies that have similarities to those, but which would be classified more as mental strategies would include mediation, bio-feedback, relaxation, and imagery.

Meditation can be a wonderful tool for both dealing with stress and aiding in sleep. Meditating before going to bed can put us in a relaxed frame of mind and remove from consciousness all the thoughts and stressors from the day that might intrude on our ability to get to sleep. Additionally, when we awaken during the night with our mind racing over problems and worries that we can't seem to shut off, doing a little meditation is a great way to shut them off.

Meditation has been around for centuries as a part of some eastern religions, but more recently it has also been used in western cultures not in a religious sense but to relax, find peace, calm the mind, and also to heighten consciousness and focus concentration. Meditation is basically the self-regulation of attention. Through the discipline of meditation we can focus our attention on an object, a thought, a process, or an awareness.

"Mindfulness" meditation is where we focus attention on the field or the background. We sit quietly and focus on an object like a candle, or a process like deep breathing. Our focus may shift from one thing to another and that is alright, but the intent is to stay in the present, not allow the mind to drift into thoughts about the past or the future.

"Concentrative" meditation is where we focus on one object, process, mantra, koan or riddle, etc., but the intent is to remain focused on that one object or that one process. We do not let our focus shift from one thing to another but always return to the specific object of our attention.

Whichever style of meditation is used, it takes practice and discipline. It is a learned process. Once we begin to master the art of mediation, however, it is a wonderful tool for managing stress.

Bio-feedback is another helpful strategy for managing stress. Bio-feedback was originally developed in the 1960's with the intent of helping people get in touch with the physiological responses they experienced in relation to stressful events. Such physiological responses include heart rate, blood pressure, breathing rate, etc. By receiving feedback on these physiological responses the individual learns to alter them utilizing deep breathing and concentration. The result is an ability to reduce one's stress response at will. Hence, it can be an effective strategy for managing stress. There are sites that sell bio-feedback equipment and sites that offer training in learning the process for those who are interested.

Relaxation is another stress reduction technique. There are multiple types of relaxation techniques. These include autogenic relaxation, progressive muscle relaxation, and visualization techniques...which will be discussed separately. Autogenic refers to something that comes from within us. We might repeat certain words or phrases or thoughts over and over to achieve relaxation. We might, for example, imagine that the head is becoming very heavy. We might imagine that the arms are very heavy and warm and are sagging into the mattress. We might imagine the sensation of sinking into warm water and how that engulfs and relaxes us. There are numerous web sites to learn autogenic relaxation for anyone interested.

Progressive muscle relaxation is where we progressively relax the muscles in the body until we achieve a state of total relaxation.

We've mentioned progressive muscle relaxation as a physical strategy, but it is also a mental strategy. To review, we may start by tensing the muscles in the feet and holding them tense for a period. Then we relax those muscles and notice the difference between the state of tension and the state of relaxation. Then we do the same with the calves. Then we progress to the thighs. We move throughout the body including the neck, face and head until we have relaxed every muscle group. This is an excellent way to reduce stress and/or to attain sleep.

Both autogenic and progressive muscle relaxation techniques are available on CDs. Listening to such a CD before bed is a great way to reduce stress and put yourself to sleep. I highly recommend having this in your arsenal of stress reduction/sleep aid techniques.

Visualization is another stress reduction technique. Visualization involves forming mental images and taking a visual journey to a real or imaginary place. This may be a sea shore, or a garden, or a special place by the lake, etc. We can visualize the sun rising or setting over the water, sea gulls floating on updrafts, waves gently crashing against the rocks or the beach. We can also imagine the sound of the waves crashing and the sound of the sea gulls. We can imagine the gentle breeze on our skin, the warmth of the sun on our face, or the feel of the sand between our toes. We might smell the ocean or scents coming in off the ocean. Such visualizations are often referred to as guided imagery, and again, are available through multiple CD options.

Schedule Time for Yourself

The last mental strategy for managing stress is very simple... putting yourself on your schedule. We put so many events, issues, and problems on our schedule that often we don't make room for putting a little "self" time in there. Taking time for ourselves is critical. That may be different for each of us, but scheduling time for ourselves is what gives us the energy to address all those other issues. When we don't make time for ourselves we burn out. In planning how we will use our time, we need to make it a habit to include a little time that refreshes us. Enjoy that time. Make the most of it. Savor it. This is what gives us the strength to face all the other issues and stressors in life.

In Summation

There are a number of mental strategies that we can use to manage and reduce stress. These include:

1. Recognizing and Avoiding Stressors—Know what causes your stress...people, places, events. Evaluate your job. What are the expectations? Are there areas where you could use additional knowledge or training? How do the climate and culture of the workplace impact your stress? Evaluate your level of emotional intelligence. Work on building emotional intelligence if necessary, and work on building relationships. Recognize the issues you can control and the issues you cannot control.

2. Addressing Mindset and Perception—Do you believe your abilities are set or that they can be developed? This is a crucial question. If necessary work on developing a growth mindset. Learn to tackle issues one at a time.

3. Analyzing and Reframing Assumptions—What assumptions do you make about others and about yourself? Are you generally optimistic or pessimistic? This is learned and, like any habit, can be changed by learning different thought habits.

4. Affirmations—By first understanding our habitual thinking, we can then replace that thinking with more positive thinking, e.g., affirmations. The way to change a habit is not to fight it or attempt to not do it, but rather to replace it with a better habit. This is what affirmations do. Challenge the automatic negative thoughts you have and replace them with positive, workable thoughts.

Gary R. Plaford

5. Problem Solving—Step back. Determine what the problem is. Brainstorm all the possibilities. Determine what outcome you want. Decide which action possibility will most likely get you want you want. Just do it.

6. Goal Setting—Look at what goals you have, what is really important to you. Are they health and wellness goals, education or achievement goals, family or relationship goals, financial or security goals, balance between career and family goals, community or philanthropic goals, travel or adventure goals, personal or other goals? Rank your goals in order of importance to you. This allows you to spend your time with what is important rather than on all the trivia.

7. Self-confidence/Self-esteem—Evaluate your level of self-confidence. Self-efficacy is gained through mastery experiences, vicarious experiences, social persuasion, and emotional status. In practice this means focusing on our successes and setting up successful experiences, learning success through watching others, surrounding ourselves as much as possible with people who are both successful and supportive of us, and establishing and maintaining a positive attitude and outlook. A good blue print for building self-confidence is to establish good relationships; find, learn, decide what is important to you; practice the skills necessary until you begin to see mastery, improvement, success; and be open to recognizing what you have achieved and accepting praise and recognition from others.

8. Meditation, Bio-feedback, Relaxation, Imagery—Select, develop, and utilize at least one of these strategies for your personal arsenal in managing stress.

9. Schedule Time for Yourself—Taking time for yourself is critical. You cannot be at your best in dealing with issues, dealing with others, or supporting others unless you take the time to revitalize yourself.

CHAPTER 9

Emotional Strategies for Managing Stress

Success is not about not failing. It is about getting up and trying again every time we fail. If we want to learn to ice skate we will fall down, quickly and often. Every fall is in itself a failure. But if we get back up one more time than we fall down we will eventually learn to ice skate, or do algebra, or read, or play the piano, or do whatever it is we want to learn to do. Success is never about not failing. Failing is part of the equation. Success is about getting back up.

As with mental strategies, there are a number of emotionally based strategies we can utilize to control, manage, and/or reduce our stress. These would include, first and foremost, understanding where stress is coming from. Is it coming from the novelty of a situation, the unpredictability of the situation, our sense of lack of control in the situation, or a threat to our ego which can be real or symbolic? A second very basic strategy is to understand a little about how the brain works and how we can actually shift the locus of control at will. A third strategy involves recognizing and reframing emotional triggers. A fourth strategy is to learn to manage our anger. Learning calming cues related to places, people, and activities is a fifth strategy. A sixth strategy is to learn patience. A final strategy is to have a plan in mind...understanding and utilizing the relaxation response.

Novelty, Unpredictability, Lack of Control, Threat to Ego

In chapter 3 we discussed the concepts of novelty, unpredictability, lack of control, and threat to ego. All the stress that we face in life comes from one, or a combination of these factors. Looking at them one at a time, novelty refers to novel situations. Change is a perfect example of novelty. How do we react to change? Stress is a common result of change, even if the change is something we wanted and looked forward to. So how do we deal with change to reduce the stress that invariably comes with the change?

Whenever we go into a new situation or know that we will be going into a new situation the first step is to be as prepared as possible for the change, the novelty. This means we must learn as much as we can about the new situation. A new job is a good example. How are things done here? Who will we be working with or for? What are they like? What support exists and where can we go for help? It also means physically touring the new environment. Knowing exactly where our office is or where we will be working, where the restrooms are, where the lunch room is located. Just knowing these things, decreasing the novelty of the situation, alleviates some of the stress.

A second factor is the unpredictability of the situation. Again, learning as much as possible about the new situation and the expectations of the situation is critical. What is expected in this situation or on this job? What are the consequences if this happens or if that happens? What happens next? Who do we report to? When do we report to them? Learning what to expect is critical.

Often novelty and unpredictability go hand in hand, but not always. It is possible to be in a situation where you know the job, you know what to predict, but it is still novel and hence stressful. For example, we might get transferred to a new plant in a different city. We are selected because we know the job; the company just wants us to do it in a new location. In this case it might be more the novelty of the new place, the new city that generates stress. Sometimes it might be the unpredictability and not the novelty of the situation that is stressful. An example could be when we remain in the same job but a new boss is hired as our supervisor. We know the expectations of our job, but the novelty of working with someone new is stressful. The point is we often see novelty and unpredictability together, but we can experience them separately.

We see examples of this every year in public education; kindergarten and some first grade students who are entering school for the first time, new sixth or seventh grade students entering middle school, or ninth grade students entering high school. Often these students are anxious, nervous, and stressed out because of the novelty and unpredictability of the situation.

In today's society many children experience pre-school in some form or another, but still some do not. For those who do not, kindergarten is the first school experience they face. What we see every year on the first day of school with some of these students is a meltdown in the hallway outside of their classroom. The student is crying, clinging to mom's legs, his hands are clutching her skirt, he is pleading with her not to leave him; mom is crying because of his distress; the teacher is telling mom to leave and just let her deal with it. This is occurring because of the novelty and unpredictability of the situation. This is one of the basic reasons schools began having open houses for parents and students before the beginning of the school year. If students see the school, see the classroom, walk around the classroom, sit at a desk, meet the teacher, do a little project the teacher has prepared like coloring a picture of the school, etc.; this addresses the novelty and unpredictability of the situation. The student knows what the room is like, what the teacher is like, the teacher is not a complete stranger, they know a little about what to expect in the classroom. The novelty and unpredictability are reduced and the stress goes down. The student may still be a little stressed the first day, but usually not enough for the hallway meltdown.

Schools also learned that some students, on the first day of school, are afraid of the big yellow school bus. It pulls up to the curb on their street, opens the doors, and suddenly the kindergarten or first grade student is terrified of getting on the bus. Mom ends up driving them to school and walking them down to the classroom.

This is why some schools have begun having a bus available at the open house. They encourage parents to take their child out onto the bus, let them climb the steps, let them walk up and down the aisle, let them sit in a seat, let them meet a bus driver. Again, this addresses the novelty and unpredictability of the situation and lowers their stress.

Recognizing that novelty and unpredictability are huge causes of stress, and addressing those by learning and experiencing whatever we can to reduce those is a major strategy in managing stress. The other side of the coin is to also make the effort to understand the similarities between a new situation and the old situation. We can not only look at what is novel, but at what is the same. We can look at what is unpredictable, but also at what is predictable. This also can reduce the stress, knowing that everything isn't new and everything isn't unpredictable.

Another strategy to address novelty and unpredictability is to make things in this new, unpredictable situation as familiar as possible. In other words, make the new office or the new desk, or the new workplace as homelike as possible. Put up pictures of children and family, put out familiar gadgets and tools, and take an old familiar coffee mug. Making the place seem familiar makes it feel not quite so novel and different.

A third factor to address is that of lack of control. Not being able to control a situation or fearing that we will not be able to control it is a huge stressor. This is a major factor in parenting. As children grow up they reach a certain age where the parents really cannot control them. We can control some of their comings and goings, but we really cannot control the child. Trying to do so, thinking that we can do so, becomes a major stressor for the parents. This is especially anxiety producing if the child begins making serious mistakes in life; like running with the wrong crowd, using drugs and alcohol, demonstrating a lack of interest in school and school work, etc. The parent often wants to step in and control everything, but that rarely works. At eighteen the child can legally leave home, and the closer they are to eighteen the more difficult it is for parents to control anything much less everything. The best thing parents can do is to put the work in early on to try to build a solid basis for emotional intelligence so the child will hopefully make good, healthy decisions for himself, because after a certain point the parents must give up control.

In looking at the factor of lack of control, a key then is to recognize what we can control and what we cannot control. This point has been mentioned earlier, but it is important to emphasize it here. We often spend a great deal of time and waste a lot of effort worrying and fretting over things that we really cannot control. What makes this even worse is that we then ignore the aspects of a situation that we can or could control. A critical step is to evaluate a situation and honestly determine what factors we can and what factors we cannot control. Make two lists, a controllable list and an uncontrollable list. Then put the uncontrollable list down and focus on the controllable list. Do what we can do. Focus our energy there. Once we have done all we can do, then if we want to pick up the uncontrollable list and bemoan those issues, at least we haven't ignored the factors we can control.

Ideally, when we look at the factors we cannot control, we can get to the point where we can let them go. That does not mean we don't care about the people or the issues in these factors, but it means that we recognize we cannot control these factors. The hard truth is, trying to control the factors that we cannot control often results in damaging or destroying relationships even more. This is where a tough love concept is beneficial. Sometimes we need to give a loved one the clear message that we love them but do not like their behavior, that we know we cannot change their behavior, but that if and when they are ready to do so we will be there to assist in any way possible. Then we love them and support them, but we do not enable them to continue in destructive ways by covering for them.

Giving up control, when we really have no control anyway, can be very hard to do and very stressful. However, trying to hang onto control when it really isn't ours to hang on to is even more stressful. It also becomes never ending. We really cannot control the situation yet we keep trying, and trying, and trying. The stress goes on, and on, and on.

A huge factor in giving up control is acceptance. As stated before, this is especially true when we are in high stress situations. Accepting that we have no control over certain situations, and accepting the changes that have occurred, will occur, or might occur because we have no control is a huge step. This does not mean giving up. It means accepting where we are, where we have landed, what has happened, and going on from there. Many people, as was stated in the previous chapter, have gone bankrupt and bounced back. Accepting their failure, and their lack of being able to control the factors of that failure or the factors that precipitated that failure, was the first step in bouncing back. Acceptance of failing, acceptance of lack of control, acceptance of defeat is not terminal. At least it need not be. It means accepting that this is our new starting point. In a war there are many battles. Every battle need not be won to win the war. Accepting when a battle is lost and knowing when to retreat, to take a step back, to regroup, to accept what has happened, and to plan the next step is crucial to ultimate victory. Losing any battle is hard, but it isn't terminal unless we give up.

Losing a battle is hard, but it isn't

terminal unless we give up.

Another issue related to lack of control is recognizing that other people also do this. Many people try to control things that they really cannot control. This is why we have "control freaks." Dealing with such people can also be stressful, but recognizing what is happening can help us deal with it more effectively.

A final thought on lack of control relates to planning and goal setting. Again, this has been discussed before, but it is important to mention here because planning and goal setting revolve around issues that we can control. This is a great way to address those issues and factors up front, to be pro-active about them, rather than waiting until we are stressed about them and merely reacting to them.

A final factor is threat to ego. This refers to real physical threats where we are in danger or think we might be in danger, and to symbolic threats where our ability is questioned, we are embarrassed, humiliated, disrespected, insulted, made to feel incompetent or inferior, etc. This is one of the key elements in bullying. Bullying can be either a real physical threat or more along the lines of relational aggression coming in the form of put downs, exclusion, humiliation, etc. Cyber bullying can include real physical threats, but it is mainly along the lines of relational aggression.

One way of addressing threat to ego is through building self-confidence and self-esteem, which has already been discussed. Without belaboring the point, it is important to understand that having something to feel good about, having an area where we feel competent is incredibly helpful in allowing us to weather threats to our ego.

Another issue related to threat to ego is to recognize where our feelings are coming from. Are they coming from what the other person said or did to us, or are they coming from inside us? Our feelings are based not on external events, the other person's actions, but rather on our interpretation of those events. The other person can treat us badly, but they cannot make us mad or sad. We make ourselves mad or sad. If we allow the other person's actions to make us mad or sad then we are giving them incredible power over us. If we do that, if we hand over the control of our emotions to other people, then we will often suffer mercilessly at their hands. What we cannot do is give others that control. Changing our thoughts about that aspect of emotions can be very beneficial. The old adage, "Sticks and stones can break my bones but words can never hurt me," is very true unless we allow those words to hurt us. We rule our own emotions unless we abdicate that rule. This is an important concept to keep in mind.

Another strategy regarding threat to ego is to always have a plan of action in mind. In the case of dealing with a bully or a situation where threat to ego is a recurring issue, having a plan in mind to deal with it is important. When this happens, this is what I will do, this is my plan. In teaching children to deal with potential sexual abuse, for example, we have taught them to have a three step plan. The plan was to "Say no, Get away, and Tell someone." Thinking through our responses beforehand, having a plan of action, takes some of the stress out of the situation. It also helps us to think in terms of "afterward." In other words, that the bullying event, for example, is not the end of life as we know it, that there is a tomorrow and this is what I will do tomorrow or after the event. It helps us put things in a little different perspective and takes some of the anxiety out of it.

Brain Functioning

A second emotional strategy for managing stress resides in understanding a little about brain functioning. In chapter four we discussed the locus of control and how it shifts in the brain. If we are addressing novel issues the locus of control is basically in the right hemisphere of the brain. If we are doing routine tasks the locus shifts to the left hemisphere. If emotions are involved, especially strong emotions or high stress, the locus shifts to the limbic system, the emotional center of the brain. The fact that the brain does this naturally is fairly new information, but this new information allows us to understand how we can manage our own emotional states by shifting the locus of control.

As discussed in chapter four, we do some of this shifting naturally. For example, in basketball some free throw shooters go through a set routine while standing at the free throw line before they shoot. Their routine might consist of dribbling the ball twice, spinning the ball in their hands, looking at the rim, dribbling once more, taking a deep breath, and then finally launching the shot.

The point is, although the free throw shooter may not know what is going on in the brain, they know that they hit more free throws when they go through this set routine. The routine is really an attempt to shift the locus of control out of the limbic system, where stress is possibly taking over, to the left hemisphere. The goal is to let the body do what it has learned to do.

Understanding how the brain works in this regard is significant. It means we can utilize routine to lower stress and allow our mind and body to function as we want them to function. In the case of sports there are many situations where this can be useful. Shooting free throws is one. Hitting a golf shot is another. Stepping into the batter's box in baseball is another. Preparing for a dive off the diving platform is yet another. Rifle competitions or archery competitions are others. The list of possibilities where this could be useful for athletes is endless.

Setting and going through routines would also be valuable in any type of performing art. Playing the piano at Carnegie Hall, singing or acting on stage, making a speech, these are all situations where utilizing routines would calm us.

Understanding that the locus of control can be shifted from the limbic system to the left hemisphere is obviously helpful in sports and performance related situations, but it is also valuable in numerous other ways. In chapter four we also discussed how language is a routine function for adults and for children past a certain age. In other words, once we have learned a language, the locus of control when we speak is in the left hemisphere. This means that talking is a routine function for adults, which is why talking things out has a calming function. Talking things out shifts the locus of control to the left hemisphere. This is important to understand. If we are upset, if we are angry, if we are anxious then talking things over, putting things into words can calm us down. It begins to shift the locus of control to the left hemisphere.

One of the noticeable differences between men and women is this notion that women tend to talk about the issues on their mind. If something is bothering them they talk about it. They talk it over with friends or they may talk it over with spouses, but they talk it over. Men sometimes think that when the women in their life want to talk about an issue they want help with that issue or want a solution for the issue. Quite often that is not the case at all. Women merely want to be heard. It is the talking about the issue that is calming, that will help them deal with it.

Men, on the other hand, often go into a cave when they face a problem. They don't talk about it, they merely think about it. Many men don't understand that talking about a problem does not mean that they need help with the problem or that they want advice regarding the problem. What talking about a problem does is to shift the locus of control to the left hemisphere. It has a calming effect so that we can more easily resolve the issue for ourselves. Men often hang onto emotions longer because they don't talk things out. When angry they stay angry, when frustrated they stay frustrated, when stressed they remain stressed. Men generally could learn a lot from women in this regard; talking things out, putting issues into language, expressing what is going on with us verbally is a tremendous strategy for managing stress. It isn't a weakness.

Another way we can introduce routine into our lives as a stress management tool is to work on organizational skills. Getting organized, and more importantly staying organized is all about routine. It takes getting into a routine to keep our lives and the things in our lives organized. Learning to put things away when we are finished with them, putting clothing away in the closet or in drawers in an orderly fashion, cleaning up after ourselves, keeping our desk or work place neat and orderly, these are routines that can be learned and utilized. They are not glamorous, but they are effective. If we can find things when we need them, that lowers stress. How much stress do we create in our lives because we have a task to do, but first we must find the tools we need before we can even begin the task? That can become frustrating and overwhelming in itself. That can cause us to walk away from completing a task just because we cannot find what we need to accomplish the task. Learning to be organized takes a little effort, but it certainly pays off in stress reduction.

Finally, routine involves problem solving skills. We discussed learning problem solving skills in the last chapter as a means of avoiding stress, but it also needs to be mentioned here as a way to manage stress. Things happen in life that might cause us to go into fight or flight, to become angry and belligerent or to run from a situation, to lash out at others or to cower in trepidation. In those situations, if we have developed problem solving skills, then we can use those skills instead of becoming angry and belligerent or running away. Having the knowledge inside us that we have the tools necessary to handle problems when they arise means we don't have to over-react. The point is, problem solving skills involve a routine way of looking at issues and solutions. These are the routine steps we take when things go wrong. That is calming. That reduces stress. It is all about routine.

Recognizing and Reframing Emotional Triggers

A third emotional stress management strategy involves recognizing and managing our emotional triggers. What is it that sets us off? What is it that makes us angry? For some people there may be certain types of situations that set them off. It may be that change is something they just don't cope well with and whenever they face change they have difficulties. It may be that they do not do well when they feel that they don't have control in a situation. It also may be that they find some specific situations difficult. For some of us going home to visit parents creates real stress. It isn't that we don't love our parents, but that being around them triggers old feelings and responses that quickly bring back all the stress of bygone years. It also can be that certain people trigger a stress response in us. Some people just seem to push our buttons.

A lot of the people and situations that trigger stress in us do so because of past events. We responded in certain ways to these people or types of people, or to these situations. We developed habitual ways of thinking about them. In other words, we developed habitual thought patterns. We have habits in how and what we think in given situations.

An example, which was mentioned earlier, is that of road rage. Certain situations with other drivers trigger a response that ends up as road rage. But the road rage does not appear overnight. Things happen while driving that are irritating or even dangerous. The person broods over this, has an internal conversation about how this is wrong and unacceptable. It happens again and again. The thoughts keep coming; the internal dialogue grows in animosity and irritability. Eventually when this happens the thoughts tip over the edge and road rage is manifested. The point is, it didn't just suddenly happen, it built up over time. What allowed it to build up was the habitual negative thoughts relating to the issues seen in other drivers.

In dealing with road rage, or dealing with anything that has become a negative emotional trigger for us, we need to recognize what it is that is triggering this response, and recognize what thoughts we are having in connection to this response. It isn't just the behavior we need to address, it is the habitual thoughts we are having that lead to or allow the behavior. It is the habitual thinking that actually triggers the emotional response, in this case the road rage.

One of the best ways to begin to deal with triggers is to first recognize what it is that triggers certain responses in us. A good way to do that is to keep a log. Write down when the negative response occurs, what were the circumstances, the who, what, when and where. But we also need to write down what thoughts we were having in connection to the event. What was it that we were thinking before this response happened? Those thoughts, that habitual thinking is the link...the trigger to the emotional response we are having.

The next step, once we realize what situations, events, or people evoke this response in us and what the habitual thinking is that is connected to our emotional response, is to change our thinking. Knowing what situations cause a negative response means we can prepare beforehand whenever we are going to face one of those situations. If it is a trip home to visit parents, then think about the visit beforehand, don't just let the emotions happen. Develop some affirmations, some positive thoughts, to replace the habitual negative ones. Also, plan some exit strategies, some times and ways to get away from the situation for just a little while to allow ourselves to calm down, to process, to regroup.

When the negative thoughts we are having and the negative responses to those thoughts are more deeply entrenched or become more serious in nature, then we can take the reframing process a step further. This is termed cognitive restructuring. Some therapies that derive from this are Cognitive Behavioral Therapy or Rational Emotive Therapy. The steps in cognitive restructuring involve identifying the problematic or "automatic thoughts;" identifying the distortions, biases, and faulty logic behind these thoughts; rationally disputing these thoughts; and developing more rational thoughts and affirmations to take their place.

With cognitive restructuring there are basically six types of automatic thoughts discussed. The first type is self-evaluative thoughts, or how we see ourselves. The second type concerns thoughts about the evaluation of others, or how we think others see us. The third type of thoughts is evaluative thoughts about others, or how we see them. The fourth type concerns thoughts about coping strategies, or what our plans are to address the situation. The fifth type of thought is about avoidance, or how can we avoid this situation rather than deal with it. The sixth type would be miscellaneous thoughts, thoughts that don't fit into the other categories.

We all have these little dialogues with ourselves, these little ongoing monologues about ourselves, others, situations, etc. Recognizing when they are negative and leading us into further negative thoughts and behaviors is important. Recognizing whether these habitual thoughts are typically about how we see ourselves, how we think others see us, how we see others, how we are planning to cope and the efficacy of those plans, or are we planning to avoid the situation or run from it in some manner is a big step in altering those thoughts. The point is we can change those inner dialogues with more positive thinking and affirmations.

Anger Management

Another emotional strategy for managing stress is to learn some anger management techniques. First of all we must understand that anger is a normal human emotion. It helps us respond to a threatening situation. It can also be a powerful motivating force if channeled properly. It is also important to keep in mind that we all get angry, but it is not the anger that causes a problem. It is the display of anger, the outbursts, the hostility, the aggression that cause the problems. These displays can be very destructive to ourselves, others, and relationships with others when they are not managed or controlled. Managing anger and the anger displays consists of first understanding what causes our anger. Secondly, we must try to reduce our angry reactions. Third, we must be able to control our anger when we do experience it.

There are some universal causes of anger. Experiencing frustration related to attaining our goals is a typical cause of anger. Feeling hurt, physically or emotionally, is often a cause of anger. Feeling like we are being harassed, put down, or disrespected in some way is a common cause of anger. Being personally attacked, either physically or mentally, is another typical cause for anger. Sensing a threat to the people, things, or ideals that we hold dear is another common cause of anger. There are other issues that may cause anger at times, but the five cited above are fairly common.

Understanding anger, however, is not merely about understanding that it might come from one of these situations. Understanding anger is about understanding why this issue causes us to feel angry. What is it that causes us to interpret someone's remarks as a threat, when another person hearing the same comments does not interpret it as a threat and become angry? The truth about anger is that it is not caused by other people or events, but rather that we choose to be angry or allow ourselves to become angry. Our anger over a situation comes from how we interpret that situation.

Here again, a good way to understand what it is that makes us angry is to keep a log. Write down the episodes that make us angry. But don't just write that this happened and therefore we got angry, write down the thoughts we had before we became angry and in connection to that anger. Identifying the thinking that leads us to anger is really where we will begin to understand where our anger is coming from.

The second step in anger management is to reduce our angry reactions. Once we understand where our anger is coming from, the next logical step is to address those situations so that they don't make us angry or as angry. Just being ready for the possibility is a big step. Knowing that a situation is developing that typically causes us anger gives us the option of potentially avoiding the situation, or at least being prepared in advance to handle the situation. This allows us to more easily take advantage of our problem solving skills, to plan some exit strategies or time out strategies, to use cognitive restructuring and be prepared with some different thoughts and affirmations related to the situation. Using these techniques and skills can help us reduce the possibility of having an angry outburst.

The third step in managing anger is to try to manage the anger when we do experience it. There are a number of strategies that can be helpful here. The first is to utilize routines. A routine could be as simple as counting to ten before we respond. It could be taking three deep breaths before we respond. It could be reciting a specific affirmation to ourselves before we respond. All of these examples delay our response, they give us time to calm ourselves just a bit before acting or responding in a manner that we later regret. These routines are habits, and as such they must be practiced before we can expect ourselves to actually use them. Having a routine or a habit that we exercise before we allow ourselves to respond can be a very effective tool.

A second strategy involves learning to communicate better. This means learning to use verbal communication as opposed to reacting physically. Using language, as has been mentioned before, is routine behavior and it helps us shift the locus of control to the left hemisphere. That alone can reduce the possibility of a physical or hostile outburst. Communicating better also means learning to express what we are feeling. A good technique is to learn to use "I" statements. An example of an "I" statement would be, "I feel

_____ when you _____ because _____." Filling in the blanks could go like this, "I feel angry when you tell me what to do because it feels like you don't have confidence in my ability to do the right thing." Learning a simple technique like "I" messages can help us express in language what it is that is making us angry and thereby reducing the need to display that anger with physicality or hostility.

A third strategy is to learn some assertiveness skills. This may initially sound like a bad strategy when talking about anger, but it can be very helpful. There is a distinct difference between being assertive and being aggressive or passive aggressive. Being assertive involves recognizing and having respect for our own personal boundaries, and standing up for those. If we can learn to be assertive, to tell others what it is that is bothering us, to get that out there in the open, then there is a much reduced need to eventually become aggressive because we are being overlooked or frustrated in our wishes.

A fourth strategy involves taking a time out or changing our environment. This could mean getting away from the situation or the individual for a period of time. This could be done by going for a walk, taking a coffee break or a restroom break, or merely getting away to do something that takes our mind off the situation. Keeping in mind that we can utilize a "time out" when we need to calm or settle ourselves is a valuable tool.

A fifth strategy is to get the anger out. That doesn't mean let the anger out in a display of hostility and aggression, but it does mean not to bottle it up. Find a release for the anger. There is a difference between expressing anger and suppressing anger. Suppressing it for an extended period of time can allow it to fester inside us, and it can be destructive to our mental and physical health. Exercise is a great way to get it out. Take a walk, go for a run, play tennis, etc. These are excellent ways to get it out. Talking it out is also helpful. Finding someone who will listen and be supportive is a great way to get it off our chest, to release the pent up pressure.

A final strategy is to learn to let it go. There are situations in life when things happen that are just not fair and just not right, but that we can really do nothing about. We can hold onto the anger and hostility related to those situations, we can take it out on others including family and loved ones or strangers, and we can beat ourselves up indefinitely if we choose to, but we really can do nothing to change the situation. When we find ourselves in that kind of a situation it is truly best to learn to just let it go. Let the situation go, let the anger go, just forget about it. Learn to put it behind us. I am not saying to be a doormat. There are situations that are unfair that we can do something about, and when we face those we need to do something about them. We need to stand up for ourselves and be assertive when appropriate. But when there is nothing that can be done, that is the time to let it go. Letting it go, putting it behind us sometimes involves forgiving others. Learn to forgive and move on. We do ourselves a horrible disservice by hanging onto the emotions and thoughts of unwinnable, unchangeable situations.

Learning Calming Cues

One of the issues we face today related to stress is that sometimes it seems to be constant, we can't get away from it. Part of this is due to technology. We all have cell phones so we are reachable whenever and wherever we are. This is one of the reasons cyber bullying can be so devastating, teens take their cell phones with them wherever they go and they are perpetual targets for the cyber bullies. There is no safe haven from it. It can get to them anytime of the day or night wherever they are. The same thing is true of our work. We can be away at a conference, at lunch, on our day off and we get a call from the office about something that needs our attention now.

In fact, between the instant communication of our computers via email or face book, and our cell phones and texting, everything has become an issue that needs immediate attention. It wasn't that long ago when much of what was done in offices was done via the mail. We received a letter about an issue, thought about it, wrote a letter back, etc. It took time to resolve issues. We had time to think it over, revise our thoughts, plan for it, etc. Now we get an email and an immediate response is expected. So we respond and get an immediate response back. Decisions are made immediately and everyone wants a decision immediately. We may get a lot more done but the price paid is that there is also a great deal more stress.

The old adage comes to mind, "All work and no play...." The point is we cannot function like that. We cannot work all the time. We cannot always be "on." The stress that generates takes a tremendous physical and emotional toll. Alvin Toffler years ago developed what was termed stability zones. He discussed stability zones in terms of people, places, things, ideas, and organizations. I would like to add one more to that list, activities. Stability zones refers to people, places, things, ideas, organizations, and activities that calm us, that offer a safe place, that become cues that de-stress us.

People can be calming cues or stability zones. These can be family members, friends, or co-workers. They are people with whom we feel comfortable. They typically have the same or similar values and beliefs. They are people we can talk to and express what we really think and really feel. We don't have to act around them. We don't have to be "on" around them. It is valuable to identify people in our lives who fit this category. If they don't exist, then it would be valuable to develop some relationships that do fit. Once we identify such people, nourish those relationships and use those relationships. That doesn't mean use them in a bad way, we may also be that other person's stability zone.

Places can also be stability zones or calming cues. Home is probably the most often noted cite that calms us. Once we are home we can relax, we can let our hair down so to speak. Calming cues might be more specific than even being at home. It could be a favorite room at home, or it could be a place like the bath tub that really calms us. For some people their office is that place where they feel most relaxed. When that is the case, unfortunately, that may not necessarily be a good sign. However, making the office or workplace a little more like home is often done to help build stability or calming into the work site. Places that are also stability zones for some could include being in the country, being at the summer home, being at the beach, being on the golf course, being at the club or being on the yacht. Again, what is important is to know what places are calming cues for us and use those to calm ourselves, to relax, to de-stress ourselves.

Things can also be calming cues. Young children have teddy bears, but even for adults having a favorite possession or something that is linked to good feelings or good times can act as a calming cue. Things that could be calming cues might include family photos, a favorite car, a bicycle, a new set of golf clubs, a favorite pair of pajamas, a blanket, something that belonged to someone dear to us, memorabilia from a special event or experience. Any of these things might be calming cues. Identifying things that can have such a calming effect on us is valuable.

Ideas could be calming cues or offer stability zones. For some people this might be in the form of religious beliefs, or an ideology, or specific values that we have. For others it might be a specific cause, like saving wild animals, preserving nature, saving the environment, etc. When such ideas exist as calming cues they can certainly be utilized to achieve those ends.

Organizations can become stability zones or calming cues. This could be in the form of belonging to a certain church, a certain club, a political party, having membership in a specific group or community organization. These can be good places to experience stability zones and also to find other people with whom relationships could be developed that offer stability zones or calming cues.

Finally activities can become calming cues and be used as such. Activities might include playing golf, walking, biking, practicing yoga or Tai-chi, sailing, dancing, knitting, reading, or any of multiple hobbies that exist. Having activities that serve as stability zones or calming cues is a huge benefit. It gives us something to focus on, to look forward to. It gets us away from the stressors and the thoughts about those stressors. If we do not have such activities it is a great idea to try to find and develop some.

Once we find or determine what our personal stability zones or calming cues are, it is a good idea to invest time in them. Nurture the relationships with those people who are our stability zones. Maintain the places and things that serve as calming cues. Support and participate in the ideas and organizations that serve as stability zones. Finally, practice the activities that provide calming cues... keep them fresh. Having and using such stability zones or calming cues is becoming even more important as technology continues to change and continues to try to make us instantly accessible and immediately responsive to the worries and troubles of our world.

Patience

Patience is often described as a virtue, but it is a virtue most of us have to build. If we were asked to describe the typical signs of impatience we might include such things as shallow breathing, muscle tightness or tension, hand clenching, restlessness or an inability to stand still, irritability and quick temper, anxiety and nervousness, rushing things and making snap decisions. If we were asked to describe the typical signs of stress we might come up with the exact same list. Impatience quickly turns into stress.

When considering patience I am reminded of the story of the boy who found a butterfly cocoon and took it to his father. The boy asked his father what it was and the father replied that it was a butterfly cocoon. He told his son that if he watched it he might see a butterfly eventually emerge from that cocoon. The boy took the cocoon to his room and watched it every day. One day an opening appeared and a butterfly began to struggle out of the cocoon. After a while the butterfly stopped. The boy, wanting to assist the butterfly, got a pair of scissors and opened the cocoon for the butterfly. Shortly the butterfly was out of the cocoon but it looked funny. The butterfly had a swollen body and shriveled wings. The butterfly never changed and eventually died. The boy was disappointed and went to his father to tell him what had happened. The father told his son that the mistake was in being impatient and helping the butterfly get out of the cocoon. The struggle to get out is what forces fluid out of its body and into its wings. The struggle is what makes it stronger, strong enough to fly. The same is true of many issues we face. Having the patience to let something happen rather than trying to force it, this is most often the best policy. It is the struggle that makes us stronger. It is the patience we develop through the struggle that builds character.

One key in addressing our own patience vs. impatience continuum is to look at the internal dialogue we are having regarding the issue at hand. Why does this have to be done immediately? What are the consequences if it is not? Is it a real crisis or is it merely my crisis? Can I back off on the deadline I have imposed? Could it be done later? Some issues we face really do need to be done right now without exception, but some do not. Sometimes the deadlines we put on ourselves or those around us are merely habit. Making that distinction and backing off when we can will reduce stress for everyone involved.

Another key is to manage our impatience by addressing the symptoms of impatience. One symptom is shallow breathing. To address shallow breathing we can try to take very slow, deep breaths. This slows down the heart rate. Another symptom is muscle tension. We can locate the muscles that are tense in our body and relax those muscles. This tension may be present in various parts of the body and it is important to try to relax each muscle or muscle group affected. Another symptom we often see is having clenched hands or fists. A good strategy is to get a stress ball and squeeze it to reduce the hand clenching. Yet another symptom is restlessness or inability to stand still. We can do a little jogging in place or go up and down on our toes to relieve this symptom. Irritability and having a quick temper is another symptom. This involves other people, so one strategy is to learn and practice active listening and empathetic listening. In other words, we don't merely wait our turn to speak but really listen to what others are saying. Only when we really listen can we really understand where the other person is coming from, and when we make the effort to do so we improve communication. It takes practice but it is well worth the effort to develop this skill.

Gary R. Plaford

Another symptom is anxiety and nervousness. As mentioned before, here is where it is good to look at the internal conversation we are having and determine what messages are valid and what messages are not. Also, it is important here to truly consider what we can control and what we cannot control and to let go of those things we really cannot control. Another symptom is that we rush things. The key strategy is to slow down. Forcing ourselves to move in slow motion is beneficial. Slowing down allows us to not merely react but to become more proactive. The little time we give ourselves by slowing down allows the brain that added time to process, and that also can be very valuable. A final symptom is making snap decisions. Slowing down helps deter this. Also, making it a rule that we will use rational problem solving strategies when making decisions rather than being forced into using behavior or garbage can models of decision making as discussed in the last chapter. Those often lead to poor decisions.

Patience truly is a virtue. Having patience can reduce our own level of stress as well as the stress of those around us. In our current world where technology can often change faster than we can turn around, where everything seems to become more and more complex, where our world can quickly look like a three ring circus, patience seems to be harder to come by and even more of a virtue for those who attain it.

Planning Ahead

A final emotional strategy for dealing with stress is to plan ahead. Emotions happen in our lives. Crises occur. People we love die. People we care about leave. Things we planned for fall apart. Yet every time something like that happens we react like it is totally and completely unexpected. The point is we need to expect it. I don't mean that we should expect the worst, but that we need to plan ahead so that we have strategies in place when the worst happens.

A plan might include telling ourselves to be patient, to back away from the issue briefly and give ourselves time and space to think it through; to utilize one of the calming cues, the people, or places, or activities that calm us; to look at what it is about the event that is causing the stress, and to determine if there are routines and what routines we can utilize to calm ourselves; to recognize if the stress is from one of our triggers and if so what rethinking and reframing can help; to use anger management techniques if necessary.

It is also important to write our plan down on an index card and put it in our wallet or purse. Have it quickly accessible and the next time something stressful happens pull it out and read it over. When highly emotional things happen in life it can become difficult to focus, difficult to recall what we thought we might do in such circumstances. During a crisis is the worst time to make a plan for how to deal with a crisis. The plan needs to be made before hand, to be in place so it can be looked at and utilized when needed. During a crisis is not the time to rely on memory, because during a crisis memory is harder to retrieve. The best strategy is to have a plan or strategy in mind, have that plan written down, have it accessible and use it.

In Summation

There are a number of emotional strategies that we can use to manage and reduce stress. These include:

1. Novelty, Unpredictability, Lack of Control, Threat to Ego— Identify from which of these the stress is coming. If it is coming from novelty; learn as much as we can about the situation, make it less novel. If it is from unpredictability; learn the normal channels, learn the expectations, what is expected of us. If the novelty and unpredictability are related to a job make the new office or work station as familiar as possible with photos of family, familiar objects, etc. If the stress is from lack of control, recognize what it is that we can control and what we cannot control. Stop wasting time, effort, and focus on what we cannot control and truly focus our energy on what we can control. Set goals and make plans regarding what is within our control and learn to let go of those things we cannot control. Also recognize

that some people we deal with are control freaks. When the stress is from threat to ego, work on building up self-confidence and self-esteem. Recognize that others really cannot make us feel bad, but rather it is our decision to feel bad. Don't give others that power. Always have a plan of action in mind.

2. In some very high stress situations we have no control, and accepting that lack of control and all that it brings is the first and often most crucial step we can take in bouncing back. Acceptance does not mean defeat. Rather, it provides the opportunity and impetus for regrouping...for the next step.

3. Brain Functioning—Understand that the brain will automatically shift the locus of control based on whether we are thinking through new information, doing routine functions, or are engaged in something that is emotionally charged. Understanding that means that we can learn to shift the locus of control at will by developing routines that will calm us and shift the locus of control to the left hemisphere when we are feeling stress. Also, understand that language is a left hemisphere function for adults and hence a calming function. Learn to use language to calm ourselves...learn to talk things out as a calming strategy. This is all about putting things into words, not asking for advice. Learning to be organized and learning problem solving skills are also great tools utilizing routine.

4. Recognizing and Reframing Emotional Triggers—Recognize those issues and situations that set us off and how they are tied in with the habitual way we think. Keep a log to help identify what sets us off and what we were thinking in relation to these issues. The key in controlling our emotions and behavior in a setting that distresses us is to control the thoughts we allow ourselves to have that lead to those emotions and that behavior. In other words we must reframe our thinking, replace those negative automatic thoughts with positive thoughts and affirmations.

5. Anger Management—Understanding what causes the anger is important. What are the conditions and what are the

thoughts we are having related to that situation that lead to the anger. Knowing what typically causes anger in us allows us to plan ahead whenever we know we will be experiencing that situation. Then we can deal with the anger by utilizing routines that calm us. We can also learn better communication and learn to express ourselves by using "I messages." We can learn and utilize assertiveness rather than aggressiveness. We can take a time out when necessary. We can get the anger out through talking or exercise rather than letting it fester. We can learn to let it go and forgive.

6. Learning Calming Cues—There are certain things that can calm us down, that make us feel safe, that allow us to actually relax and let our hair down. These calming cues or stability zones include people, places, things, ideas, organizations, and activities. Find which of these we have as calming cues and nurture, develop, maintain, and utilize them.

7. Patience—Cherish patience as a virtue and know that exercising patience actually makes us stronger. Examine the internal dialogue we have regarding deadlines. Is it a real necessity or a self-inflicted mandate? When we can, back off. Address the symptoms of impatience. Breathe deeply. Relax the tight muscles. Use a stress ball to unclench our hands. Jog in place or stretch to stop the restlessness. Practice active listening and empathetic listening to address irritability. Examine the internal dialogue to understand and address our anxiety. Honestly look at what we can and cannot control and let go of the things we cannot control so we can focus on what we actually can control. Slow ourselves down. Don't make snap decisions.

8. Planning Ahead—Be ready for emotional issues to arise, they always do. Things happen. Expect things to happen. Write down some strategies that will help us deal with emotional issues when they arise. Have these readily available. When we need them, we will have them to help us get through. During a crisis is the worst time to plan how to manage a crisis.

CHAPTER 10

Spiritual Strategies for Managing Stress

Time is the stuff life is made of. Time is free, but it is also priceless. We can't own time, but we can use it. We can't keep time, but we can spend it. And once we've lost it, we can never get it back. How we choose to use our time is how we choose to measure our lives, for "life is truly not measured by the breaths we take, but rather by the moments that take our breath away."—Hilary Cooper

We have discussed physical, mental, and emotional strategies for dealing with or managing stress. There are also spiritual strategies. Spiritually based strategies and/or spirituality is not necessarily about religion or religious beliefs. That can be a part of it and for many people it is a large part of it. But being spiritual does not equate with being religious. We can be spiritual without being religious. We can also be religious without being spiritual. Being religious without being spiritual often comes out in very negative ways, such as the infamous Spanish Inquisition or as warfare between religious ideologies. This is what we are seeing when a religion preaches hatred for other groups of people.

Spirituality is about having beliefs and values in which we can find solace. Spirituality is about having a reason to live. It involves believing that there is right and wrong, good and bad, virtue and evil. It is about having a belief that there is a reason, a purpose for being here on this earth. It is about believing that we have a purpose. Again, for many, religion is a part of all this, but for many it is not. It is quite possible to feel we have value, to believe there is a reason to exist without having a religious basis for those beliefs.

Spiritual based strategies for managing stress include using the teachings of one's own religion, but it also includes examining one's values, analyzing one's beliefs, acceptance, creating an outward focus, establishing and practicing ceremonies and traditions, looking at how we evaluate success and ultimately considering how we actually use our time.

Religious Beliefs

Using religious beliefs as a means of managing stress is very individual in nature. It, first of all, depends on what one's religion is. However, there are some similarities in most religions. Most religions speak to some degree about love, compassion and forgiveness. Finding and utilizing those teachings from one's own religion is a great place to begin in helping manage one's own stress. Love, compassion, and forgiveness are, after all, not only intended for others but for ourselves as well. The ability to love oneself, to be compassionate towards oneself and to forgive oneself are important steps in ultimately being able to manage stress.

Examining Values

A critical strategy for managing stress is to examine what it is that we really value in life. How often do we actually scrutinize what it is that we value? Our values guide our decision making. Our values are the basis for our behaviors. Yet how often do we take the time to consider what our values really are? In chapter eight we discussed goal setting. To set goals we have to know what goals are really important to us, but this goes a little further. The goals we have are really determined by what we value. Do we value family and family relationships? Do we value intimacy with one particular individual? Do we value friendships? Do we value money? Do we value security? Do we value success? Do we value education? Do we value fame and notoriety? Do we value excitement or adventure? Do we value travel?

When we get into relationships with other people, one of the biggest reasons for those relationships to fail is that the individuals in the relationship have different values. If one values family above all and the other values money or adventure above all, that ultimately leads to conflict. That leads to attempting to change the other person, giving in and going along with the other person with the hopes of eventually fulfilling our own desires, or eventually giving up and going our separate directions. Yet when we select a mate or life partner, how often do we actually scrutinize our joint values to see if there is compatibility? Often we do not. We fool ourselves into thinking that love conquers all. Sometimes love will do that, but that is asking a great deal of love because it means someone in the relationship has to change their values or ignore their true values. I'm not trying to be a downer regarding love, but ever growing divorce rates cannot be ignored.

So what is it that we value? On the values chart included take a little time to write down the things in life that are really important to you, the things you really value. You can use the ideas in the first paragraph in this section as a guide. Take your time. Be honest. Don't write down what you think you should value, but what you actually do value.

Values Chart--What Do I Value?

1.

2.

3.

4.

5.

6.

7.

8.

9.

10.

11.

12.

After doing that, go back and look at your list of values. Rank order them. In other words put a number "1" by the item that is most important to you. Put a number "2" by the second most important value, and continue until you have ranked them all. Double check your rankings and make adjustments if necessary.

Now you have a list of the values you actually possess at this point in time. Understand that your values can and do change as you age and as situations in your life change, but these are your current values. Knowing what it is you actually value is a big step in managing stress because it helps weed out the trivia and focus on what is really important to you. Too often we spend a lot of time worrying and fretting over trivia. Having this understanding is important, it is a first step. Keep this list because we will be coming back to it.

Analyzing Beliefs

Analyzing our beliefs is another spiritual based strategy for dealing with stress. What is it that we actually believe? This goes far beyond religious beliefs. Do we believe in the sanctity of life, or do we believe in the quality of life? What we believe along those lines determines whether we keep someone alive at all costs regardless of their pain and suffering, regardless of the their chances of coming back to consciousness, or whether we allow them to die or even assist them to die with dignity. Do we believe that a woman has a choice in what happens regarding her body, or do we believe that the rights of an embryo take precedent? That determines whether we support the choice for abortion or whether we believe abortion should not be a choice. Do we believe in free will and choice, or do we believe in determination and fate? What do we believe in regards to the rights of an individual vs. the common good of society? What do we believe about individual responsibility in our lives vs. finding someone to blame for every wrong? Do we believe our intelligence is set or do we believe we can influence our intelligence by what we do? Do we believe that winning is a goal or do we believe that winning is everything and the winning justifies whatever it takes to win? What we believe plays a critical part in how we behave and what we support or don't support.

We see this in a variety of issues in our society. We see serious disagreements over abortion.   We see differences of opinion regarding euthanasia and stem cell research. We see politicians and political parties who are so engaged in winning that they disregard what is really good for our country or for the people of our country. In public education we try to teach all students the same, but disregard the fact that they are coming into our schools with different beliefs about their abilities. It is no wonder some students are so hard to engage, they don't begin their educational careers with the same beliefs about their abilities or about education. Our beliefs dictate our actions.

As with our values, however, how often do we actually sit down and examine our beliefs? I encourage you to take a few minutes to think about and write down those beliefs that are the strongest, the truest, the most meaningful for you. These will include religious beliefs for many people, but they should also address some of the non-religious issues mentioned in the previous paragraphs. Our beliefs act as beacons for our decisions and our actions. These serve as a light house that guides us through the darkness over troubled waters. It is important to take the time to examine what these guiding beliefs are.

Acceptance

In the previous two chapters we have mentioned acceptance. Acceptance of what has happened, where we are, and what we cannot control is a crucial step. Acceptance is a spiritual strategy because it brings peace. Acceptance can aid in lowering our stress level from one of high stress to that of moderate or even mild stress. It calms us. Through accepting what has happened and where we now are, we can focus on what we can do as a next step. Acceptance does not equate with defeat, let's be clear on that. Acceptance allows us to realize what we cannot do and focus on what we can do.

> Acceptance allows us to realize what we
> cannot do and focus on what we can do.

Creating an Outward Focus

Another spiritual strategy for managing stress is to create an outward focus. This means getting involved with others, serving others, volunteering to help others. When we take the time to help others it takes the focus off of our own lives and our own troubles. Quite often it can help us realize that our troubles are minimal by comparison. Helping other people serves to put our own life and our own issues in perspective. Life is really all about perspective. When we step far enough away from an issue it changes our perspective of that issue. It doesn't necessarily change the issue itself, but we do see it in a different perspective, and in that regard it changes the issue for us. Volunteering to help others, to help children, to help the elderly, or even to help animals is a great way to accomplish creating an outward focus and changing our perspective. Broadening our perspective, as opposed to introspection, often serves to reduce the stress we are experiencing in our lives as well as give us purpose in life.

I love the analogy Victor Frankl gives in *Man's Search for Meaning.* He talks about how many young people are fascinated by the boomerang. They like it because it is a wonderful toy that comes back to you when you throw it. But Frankl says that is wrong. Ask any Aborigine. The boomerang is a weapon. It is designed and used for hunting. The one that comes back to us is the one that has missed the mark. If it misses, what we must do is pick it up and throw it again. What is important is what is out there, what we are throwing at, not what is lying at our feet because it missed. The focus is different. The focus is out there. When all the focus is inside, when our time is spent looking only inward, it is difficult to find our place in the world, it is difficult to see things from another perspective, it is difficult to put life in perspective, and it is difficult not to become stressed and worried when the focus is only on ourselves.

What are some good ways to develop an outward focus? There are all sorts of volunteer opportunities around. We could help build houses through Habitat for Humanity. We could volunteer at our church or place of worship. We could volunteer at a community kitchen. We could volunteer to be a Big Brother or Big Sister. We could volunteer to read to children or mentor children at a school. There are opportunities to serve on boards and committees for many social service agencies. There are opportunities to volunteer at animal shelters. Contacting a local social service agency, school, or United Way office is a great way to begin to develop an outward focus and, as a result, have a positive impact on our perceptions and sense of purpose as well as our stress level.

Establishing Ceremonies and Traditions

A sixth spiritual strategy for managing stress is to establish and practice ceremonies and traditions. Why are ceremonies and traditions important? It is because they are the building blocks for the culture of a group. They define the culture, they act as symbols for the culture, and they maintain and pass the culture along. We typically think of nationalities as having cultures. As we discussed in chapter eight, every work place has a culture. Every long standing group has a culture. Every family has a culture. A family may exhibit the over-riding culture of the nationality or country where the family resides, but all families add their own unique idiosyncrasies to their culture.

How a family celebrates Christmas, or Chanukah, or other holidays can vary greatly. For example, at Christmas does the family open gifts on Christmas eve or on Christmas morning? Do they sing carols before opening gifts? Do they all open gifts at the same time or one at a time so they can watch each other and share their experience, surprise, and joy? Do they have a special meal before or after the gift exchange? Does the gift exchange have religious overtones? Does a particular individual pass out the gifts? What stories are told about Christmas to the children? The unique ceremonies and traditions that a family has become a significant part of that family's culture, and these unique signs of the culture we belong to are calming and soothing to us. They help us relax. They reduce stress. They help us feel that we belong.

Basically, as we discussed previously, culture provides and defines boundaries for us. It delineates the group to which we belong. Culture conveys a sense of identity, it tells us who we are. Culture facilitates commitment to something larger than oneself, it gives us purpose as a member of a larger group. Culture enhances the stability of the system, it acts as the glue that holds a group together. Culture serves as a sense making and control mechanism, it guides and shapes the attitudes and behaviors of the group toward each other. These functions of culture; giving us membership, giving us identity, giving us purpose, giving us a functioning group, and giving us expectations and mores for behavior all serve as calming, stabilizing, stress reducing functions.

We see this in long standing groups. We see this in churches and in religious practices. And we see this in families. In fact, when we are individually highly stressed and/or in times of greater stress and uncertainty, what we see is individuals turning to the signs, symbols, ceremonies, and traditions of their culture. This helps us to find peace, to find predictability, to resolve confusion and to find direction. Culture is the glue that unites us with others, that provides that unity and solidarity with others, that gives us identity, that gives us purpose and that makes sense of the confusion.

When we look at the families of troubled teens, of teens who are getting into gangs and drugs, of teens who repeatedly wind up in juvenile court, what do we often see? Quite often we see families that lack ceremonies and traditions, families that have not built a culture. There is nothing special to belong to. There is no identity or membership with the family as a group. There is no solidarity. There is no purpose defined by the family. There is no guidance or direction proffered. As a result the teen seeks membership, identity and direction elsewhere. I am not saying that every teenager who gets into trouble has a family that has not built a culture. The adolescent years are difficult and any adolescent can make poor decisions. What I am saying, however, is that whenever we see families that have no ceremonies or traditions, families that have really not built a culture, those children are at much greater risk for getting involved with gangs, drugs or criminal behavior of some kind.

The point is the culture that we build, that we enforce, that we practice within a family or within any group we belong to, is important in multiple ways. These ways include the fact that it impacts the stress or the level of stress in our lives, and it impacts how we deal with or manage that stress.

So how do we build culture in a group or in a family? We use symbols that convey meaning. This could include photos of past ceremonies, family crests, recognition of members with such things as birthday cakes, awards for achievements, etc. We can use slogans and special jargon that conveys meaning. This would include the special sayings, adages, proverbs that we share with each other. Proverbs like, "Only when you can be extremely pliable and soft can you be extremely hard and strong," or, "God gives us the nuts, but he does not crack them," or "There is no pillow so soft as a clear conscience." Such proverbs convey meaning, convey attitude, convey direction and hence convey culture. Most groups have such sayings. We also use stories. Stories convey past successes or failures, and in so doing they convey the history and purpose of a culture. And, we especially use ceremonies and traditions. How do we celebrate birthdays? What do we do at special holidays? When do we get together and what holidays do we actually celebrate?

The culture that we build, the culture that we practice, the culture that we share guides our perceptions of ourselves, of our place in the group, of our purpose, of our perception of the outside world, and of how we mesh with it. Perception is everything. I'm reminded of the view offered regarding Dog and Cat theology. A dog looks at you and thinks, "You feed me, you water me, you take care of me, you must be God," and the dog is devoted to you. A cat looks at you and thinks, "You feed me, you water me, you take care of me, I must be God," and the cat is devoted to itself. It is all about perception.

Gary R. Plaford

Evaluating Success

Evaluating success is another spiritual based strategy for managing stress because evaluating success is all about having meaning and purpose in life. If we don't feel a sense of meaning and purpose then how can we possibly feel we are being successful? Everyone does not evaluate success the same way. If we could ask Mother Teresa about success we would get her take on what success is all about. If we asked Donald Trump the same question we might get a somewhat different answer. If we asked professional golfers to define what success is some might say winning the tournament, others might say finishing in the top ten and still others might say that it is making the weekend cut or keeping their playing status. We each have to define success for ourselves. The question is, how do we make that determination? How do we, as individuals, decide what success is for ourselves?

I like the way Anthony Robbins discusses how we define success. He states that there are five factors that are significant. The first factor is our emotional state of mind. The second factor relates to the questions we ask ourselves. The third factor is our values. The fourth factor is our beliefs. The fifth factor that comes into play relates to the experiences we have had.

Anthony Robbin's Five Factors in Evaluating Success

1. Our emotional state of mind

2. The questions we ask ourselves

3. The values we have

4. The beliefs we hold

5. The experiences we have had

How does our emotional state of mind affect success? For example, say we are going for an interview for a job. We get up in the morning and we get an early phone call telling us that our son got cut from the team he was trying to make. We have to give him the news. He is so devastated that he misses the bus and now we end up driving him to school. When we go out to the car we find we have a flat tire that has to be fixed before we can take him to school or get to the interview. We get the tire changed but we are a little sweaty and all we have time to do is wash our hands before rushing off to the school and our interview. We just make it into the building before the interview is scheduled to begin. Our emotional state of mind can not only affect how we do in that interview, but whether we actually care if we do well or not. Sometimes an individual's state of mind is such that they don't even show up for the interview.

Whether we have a fixed or a growth mindset, which was discussed in chapters five and eight, is another aspect of our state of mind. Whether we believe we can do something or not certainly influences success. It influences whether or not we even attempt some things, how much of an effort we make if we do attempt it, how well we do at a given endeavor, and how we evaluate what is a successful or adequate outcome to the endeavor. The state of mind we bring to any situation is a critical piece of the success we ultimately have.

The questions we ask ourselves are also critical to success. This often stems from the habitual thoughts we have which were discussed in chapters six, eight, and nine. When we fail at something do we ask ourselves something like, "Why do I always fail? Why did I do this again? Why can't I ever get it right?" Or do we ask ourselves questions like, "What did I do wrong this time so I don't make the same mistake again? How can I be better prepared so that the next time I am successful?" The habitual kinds of things we ask play a key role in performance and in success.

It isn't always habitual thinking that gets us into trouble. It's the kind of thinking or the kind of questions we are asking

Gary R. Plaford

that can lead us down a path of failure. I remember several years ago watching, as I often do, a golf tournament on television. I remember specifically watching what happened on one par three hole. On Friday afternoon K. J. Choi, who is a very good golfer and one I enjoy watching, hit a tee shot that came up short and ended up in the lake in front of the green. He ended up with a bogey. On Saturday I watched him play the same hole. This time he pulled out too much club and hit it over the green. The announcer made a comment that it was understandable that K. J. hit too much club on Saturday because of hitting it short and in the water on Friday. I cannot read minds, but I suspect that the question he was asking on Saturday was something like, "What if I hit it in the water again?" The questions we ask play a significant part in the success we have.

A third factor that is critical relates to our values. I have already discussed the importance of values in relation to stress, but our values are also critical in how we define success. Some golfers value making birdies, and will attack even difficult pin placements to get them. They may make some bogeys in the process, but their play is aggressive because they value birdies. Other golfers value par and not making bogeys. They will often play more conservative shots. Consequently they make far fewer birdies, but they also make far fewer bogeys. Both types of strategies have won golf tournaments, but the tactics used to win, to be successful, are determined by what is valued.

If an individual values family, but he spends all of his time making money and ignoring his family, how successful has he been? The world may look at him as a success because of his millions. Does his family evaluate it the same? Does he evaluate it as success?

A fourth factor critical in looking at success is what we believe. Prior to 1957 it was believed that the human being could not run a mile in under four minutes. That belief was stated by sports writers, by columnists, it was repeated on the radio and on television. It could not be done. The human body was incapable of running that fast for that long. Then, in 1957,

Roger Banister did it. He broke the four minute mile. Once he did it, suddenly people believed it was possible. Within that very year thirty seven other runners broke the four minute mile. Within the next year another hundred did it. If we believe something cannot be done, then we surely cannot do it. If, on the other hand we believe something is possible, we will often find a way to achieve it.

A final factor in success is related to the experiences we have had. Success breeds success. Likewise, failure breeds failure. In golf it is hard for most golfers to win that first tournament. Winning a second tournament is usually much easier because now we have experience on which to draw. We know what it takes. We know we can handle the emotions of the moment. We know the taste of success. Experience is not only what has happened, it is in the mind. Imagining success is part of experiencing it. If we can see it in our mind it is something we can draw on. Imagery is powerful. Experience, both actual and imagined, is a driving force in success.

Having looked at these five factors in success and how we evaluate success, Anthony Robbins asks a series of questions that force us to examine how these factors influence our thoughts and actions. The first question he asks is, "What is your most treasured memory?" Take a moment and think about that. Select one memory from your life that is your absolute favorite. Now ask yourself what factors came into play when you selected your most favorite memory. Was it your state of mind, the questions you ask yourself, your values, your beliefs, or your experiences? In this case it is probably a combination of your experiences, which are necessary for having memories, but also your values. If you value family above all, then more than likely your favorite memory has something to do with family. So in this instance, again, it would be our experiences and our values that determine the answer to that question.

Another question Robbin's asks is, "If you could end world hunger today by killing one innocent person, would you do so?" Think that over for just a few moments. If you could completely and forever end world hunger by killing one innocent person, would you do it? Now ask yourself what drives your response? In this instance you might be accessing values, the value of human life versus the value of helping mankind. You might also be accessing what you believe, is it wrong to kill or is it wrong to go on letting so many people in the world suffer from hunger? Your values and beliefs would be crucial in answering such a question.

Another of Robbin's questions is, "If you backed your car into a red Porsche and dented and scratched it, but no one was around to see, would you leave a note?" Your car is undamaged. You are positive no one saw what happened. Your insurance will definitely go up if you leave a note with your name and number. So what do you do? Do you leave a note or do you drive away without leaving a note? After thinking about what you would actually do, think about what factors are driving your decision. Values such as honesty might play a part in your decision. Beliefs might play a part. These might be a belief in right and wrong, or it could be a belief that if this individual can afford a Porsche they can certainly afford to get it fixed easier than you can. It could also be experience that comes into play. Possibly last month someone dented your car and they didn't leave a note so you got stuck with the repair bill. You might also be accessing your state of mind. For instance, maybe you just received word that your mother was in the hospital because of a horrible accident and you need to get there right away. This little dent is trivial in comparison and you just don't have the time to waste. Any of these could influence the decisions you make.

Another question Robbin's asks is "If you could earn $10,000 for eating a bowl of live cockroaches, would you?" Sounds like reality television. There they are in front of you wiggling and squirming in a bowl, and you get $10, 000 just for eating them. Would you do it? What factors would determine your response? Your experiences might be a part of it...cockroaches are filthy, yucky, disgusting creatures. Or the questions you might ask yourself, how much could I use that money? What could I do with that $10,000? Values might also play a part…how much do I value money?

Let's ask one more question. If you were home alone late one evening, and you hear something at the back door, what do you think it is? What factors are behind your thoughts? It could be experience, possibly your roommate or your spouse or partner works late and this is about the time they normally get home. Or it could be your state of mind because there have been a series of burglaries in the neighborhood, or because you just watched a horror show on television and you are frightened.

The point of this little exercise is just to demonstrate that these factors play a key role in how we evaluate events in our life. How we evaluate success, how we define what success is, and what it means to achieve success is a critical aspect of how much stress we have in our life.

Using Time Effectively

How we use our time is another strategy for managing stress. I put it under the category of spiritual strategies because it is or it should be linked closely with our values. How we use our time is the greatest demonstration we can make about what our values really are. When we discussed values earlier you were asked to write down your values and then rank order them as to which values are really most dear to you. It's time to make another list. Write down the most significant roles you play in life. We all have many roles. You may be a spouse, a parent, a son or daughter, a sibling, a grandson or granddaughter, a grandparent, an uncle or aunt, a cousin, an employee, a manager, a student, a volunteer, a sports fan, a customer, a contributor, a golfer, a biker, a jogger, etc. The point is we play many roles. It may be helpful to go back to your list of values to make sure you get all of your most significant roles.

The Roles We Play

1.

2.

3.

4.

5.

6.

7.

8.

9.

10.

11.

12.

Once you have your list of roles, rank order these by their importance to you just as you did with the list of values. In fact, it is wise to look at your values list to help determine which roles are really the most important in your life. Be honest, rank them in their order of importance, not what you think should be important.

Now add one more factor to that list. Beside each role listed write your best guess estimation of the amount of time you spend on that role. You may do so as the number of hours in an average day you might spend in that role, or you may do it as a percentage of your time, e.g., ten percent of your time is spent on this role, fifteen percent is spent on that role, etc. The point is to put your estimation in a form that makes sense to you.

Finally, look over your list. Are the roles that are the most important to you the ones where you are spending the most amount of time, or are there surprises? I have taught a number of classes on parenting over the years and quite often parents will cite the role of parent as one of the most, if not the most, important role they play in life. Yet when they look at the amount of time they actually spend parenting it is alarming to them. Now it is understandable that when you have a job and need to earn money to support a family, that will take a considerable amount of time. However, there should be some correlation between what is most important to us and how we actually use our time. For some of us, if we look at the amount of time we spend watching television we could surmise that watching television is our most valued role.

I like the perspective given by Bill Oliver in a program called "Parent to Parent." He stated that we all have things in life that are important to us and things that are not important. We also have things that are urgent to us and things that are not urgent. Things that are both important and urgent fall under the category of a crisis. If it is important to us and it is urgent then we must attend to it immediately. We cannot put it off. This is a crisis. It must be dealt with now.

Something that is important to us yet is not urgent falls under the category of creative time. This is something that is important and yet we don't have to rush it. We can take the time to plan for it and do it right. This is time when we can truly be creative and purposeful in what we do.

When something is not important to us but at the same time urgent, it would be classified as trivia. These are things that are not really important in the scheme of things but if we are going to do them we need to do them now. For example, say it is eleven-thirty A.M. on Saturday and we have some dry cleaning, some of our favorite things, that need to get to the cleaners before they close at noon if we are going to wear those clothes next week. It isn't really critical, we have other clothes that we could wear, but if we are going to do it then it must be done now. It is not important but it is urgent. We all have trivia to contend with.

Finally, there are things that are neither important to us nor or they urgent. These things fall in the category of wasted time. For example, we are sitting in front of the television switching through channels to see if there is anything that could hold our interest. This is neither important nor urgent. We all need some down time, some time to veg out, some time that is wasted time just to relax, but if we fill our day up with it, that becomes truly tragic.

	Urgent	Not Urgent
Important	Crisis	Creative Time
Not Important	Trivia	Wasted Time

If most of our time is spent in crisis mode, then we are either too busy or we are not planning ahead nearly enough. If our time is spent on trivia then we need to take a closer look at what our values really are. If most of our time is spent as wasted time, then we need to examine our beliefs closely. Is there any meaning and purpose in our life? What is truly ideal, what is truly special, is when we can take those roles that are the most significant in our life and spend creative time making those roles meaningful. If a certain relationship is important to us, then how can we use our creative energies to demonstrate that to the other person or persons? Those roles that are the most important to us should be addressed in our creative time. We don't have to merely let moments happen, we can create them, we can build them. And when we do that we find that we are happier, more content, and actually have less stress.

In Summation

There are a number of spiritual strategies for managing stress. These include:

1. Religious Beliefs—For anyone who practices a formal religion utilizing the teachings of that religion can be valuable in helping manage stress. The teachings related to love, kindness, understanding, forgiveness, and compassion are often the places to begin.

2. Examining Values—Our values guide our decisions and actions, yet we typically spend very little time examining our values. Taking a close look at what we truly value is important in so many ways. If we make the effort to align what we do with and in our lives with the values we profess to have, that alone will affect the amount of stress and the level of stress we face in life.

3. Analyzing Beliefs—The specific beliefs we have about issues, about right and wrong, and even about ourselves give us direction and purpose in life. Again, as with values, most of us spend very little time examining our beliefs, yet it is something we should take the time to do regularly throughout life.

Gary R. Plaford

4. Acceptance—Acceptance brings peace. It allows us to realize what we cannot do and focus our efforts on what we can do.

5. Creating an Outward Focus—Creating an outward focus is all about taking the focus off ourselves and looking outside ourselves. There is a time and place for introspection, but when we get caught up in introspection, in looking inside ourselves, in belly-button gazing, then we quickly lose perspective about what is important in life. We find purpose and meaning in life from looking outward, not inward. We find out who we are, we learn more about ourselves from looking outward than we ever do from introspection. Looking outward is what helps us put everything into perspective. Having perspective is key in managing stress. Volunteer, help others, get involved in the world outside.

6. Establishing Ceremonies and Traditions—Ceremonies and traditions are the means of learning, maintaining, and practicing a culture. Culture gives us identity, belonging, and purpose outside of ourselves. Culture is the glue that holds any group together. It is this belonging, this identity, this purpose that helps us manage the issues that create stress in our individual lives.

7. Evaluating Success—Our state of mind, the questions we ask ourselves, our values, our beliefs, and our past experiences are all critical aspects in how we evaluate success. Success is something we all strive for, but what is embodied in success is based on individual interpretation. The way we look at it has significant bearing on the stress we experience in life and how we cope with that stress.

8. Using Time Effectively—How we use our time is the greatest demonstration we can make of what it is in life that we truly value. We all play many roles in life, and some of those roles demand more of our time than others. At which roles do we want to spend our time, and are we taking steps to achieve that? Are we wasting much of our time, are we spending most of our time on trivia, are we in constant crisis, or are

certain roles in life significant enough that we decide to devote creative time in promoting, nurturing, and cultivating them? When we make such an effort the benefits show up in happiness, contentment, and zest for life and that certainly has a most positive affect on our ability to deal with stress.

CHAPTER 11

Where Do We Go From Here?

What is the difference between a painter and an eye doctor? The most significant difference may be in what they want us to see. The eye doctor wants us to see the world as it is. The painter wants us to see the world as he sees it. In truth, however, is there a world "as it is," a world that we all see the same? Is there one reality? Or is it that we all see our worlds through different lenses? That for each and every one of us the world we know is the one that we have built based on our different perceptions and colored by all of our past experiences and our past perceptions? If that is so, then we all see the world differently. We live in the world that we believe exists. We cannot live in another world. Hence, to live with each other effectively we must all see the world as a painter. Truly communicating with other people is not about trying to get each other to see "a" reality, but rather trying to see what the other person sees and trying to help them see what we see.

I used this thought about the painter and the eye doctor in another book, *Sleep and Learning,* but I thought it was very appropriate for the point I need to make here. I have always agreed with the point of view that working in the social sciences as a social worker, psychologist, therapist, or counselor is partially a science and partially an art. In reality this is true for all of us. Dealing with other people effectively in any milieu is partly a science and partly an art.

The science part is in the knowing and understanding. The art is in the being patient and caring enough to see what is there, what is in front of us. Painting, for example, is not really about putting something down on canvas. It is about seeing, really seeing, what is there. A summer tree is not merely green. The leaves that are in the sunlight are bright green and may sparkle with an almost silvery sheen. The leaves at the center of the tree as we peer inside may look nearly black in the deep shadows. And there are multiple shades of green in between. Unless we really see the tree we cannot put it down on canvas. Even with abstract art or impressionism the artist clearly "sees" in his mind what he intends to put down on the canvas. Painting is truly more about seeing than doing.

Likewise, unless we make the effort so really see the person we are interacting with; the good and the bad, the strengths as well as the weaknesses, the silvery parts in the sunlight as well as the darkness in the shadows we cannot truly understand and feel empathy for that person. Having facts about the other person is information, it is science. Being patient enough to see how the other person perceives those facts and hence how they perceive their world, that is art. Putting science and art together makes us better listeners, better communicators, and better friends and companions. Since this book is about stress, it is also important to point out that these factors aid us in both decreasing stress and managing stress.

In this book I have attempted to incorporate some of the science and some of the art necessary in managing stress. I have tried to provide facts and perspectives, information and insights. I feel that to effectively manage stress we must first understand stress. Hence part one in this book is all about the science of understanding stress.

We began with a discussion about what happens in the body when we experience stress, and how stress is a part of how we function and how we make decisions. It is not the antithesis of decision making and problem solving but rather a part of that process and, when considered properly, a useful part of that process.

Gary R. Plaford

Next we discussed levels of stress. All stress is not created equal. Mild stress can be motivational; it can spur us on to actions and decisions. High stress eventually can become fight or flight; which is a part of our human design aimed at helping us to survive danger, but which can also cause us major issues. We also discussed the five domains of emotional intelligence and the relationship between emotional intelligence and stress.

Then we looked at the conditions that cause stress. Every stress we face comes from one of these factors; novelty, unpredictability, lack of control, or thereat to ego. Examples were provided demonstrating how each of these causes or exacerbates stress.

In the next chapter we briefly discussed how the brain functions in relation to the locus of control. When we are thinking through something novel the right hemisphere takes over. When we are doing something routine the left hemisphere is engaged. When strong emotions are involved the locus of control can shift to the limbic system or the emotional system where fight or flight could be initiated. We discussed examples of this in both sports and everyday life. Understanding this locus of control shift provides us the potential to use this shift to our advantage in managing stress.

Following that we discussed assumptions and mindset. The assumptions we make about ourselves and the mindset we have about our abilities and even our intelligence influences how we function and even the effort we are willing to put forth. Our mindset significantly affects the stress in our lives.

The final chapter in part one covered habits and the habitual way we think. We looked at some of the automatic negative thoughts that influence our decisions and our actions. Habitual thinking means we have forged neural pathways for those thoughts. The best way to deal with habits of any kind, including habitual thinking, is not to attempt to ignore them or just not do them, but rather to replace them with more positive thoughts, more positive habits.

Part two deals with the art of how we cope with stress. Once we truly understand stress, how can we avoid it, diminish it, or manage it? In my opinion the best way of putting this in a perspective that is workable and useable is to look at it in terms of strategies. There are physical strategies, mental strategies, emotional strategies, and spiritual strategies. Why did I choose this format? I chose it because we have these for aspects of life that we deal with daily. There is the physical, the mental, the emotional, and the spiritual. Although we discussed each of these aspects separately, each and every one of these aspects influences and is influenced by each of the other aspects. However, looking at them separately is the best way to understand and develop strategies for avoiding, diminishing, and/or managing stress.

The physical strategies discussed include exercise, yoga, Tai chi, deep breathing, healthy life style, healthy diet, and proper sleep. The mental strategies include recognizing and avoiding stressors, addressing mindset and perception, analyzing and reframing assumptions, using affirmations, problem solving, goal setting, building self-confidence and self-esteem, using mediation, bio-feedback, relaxation and imagery, and scheduling time for yourself. Emotional strategies include addressing the four conditions that cause stress, using what we know about brain functioning, recognizing and reframing emotional triggers, developing anger management skills, learning calming cues, developing patience, and planning ahead. Spiritual strategies include using our own religious beliefs, examining values, analyzing beliefs, acceptance, creating an outward focus, establishing ceremonies and traditions, evaluating success, and managing our use of time.

I hope that this book is helpful in your personal journey in life. Stress is a part of life. Not all stress is bad. Stress can be motivational and push us toward initiating necessary change. When stress becomes too high or too persistent it can also cause us serious problems. Paraphrasing Joseph LeDoux, "When fear becomes anxiety, desire becomes greed, annoyance becomes anger, anger becomes hatred, friendship becomes envy, love becomes obsession, or pleasure becomes addiction, our emotions are working against us." The stress involved when this happens can become so intense that we no longer consider solving issues but rather running from issues or the reality of those issues. If we understand stress and develop the tools we need to manage stress that need not happen. Here's hoping you find the wisdom, strength, insight, and perspective, the science and the art, to address the stress in your life in a healthy and productive manner.

INDEX

BIBLIOGRAPHY

Amen, D. G. (2002). *Mind Coach: How to Teach Kids and Teenagers to Think Positive and Feel Good* Newport Beach, CA: Mindworks Press.

Bandura, A. (1997). *Self-Efficacy: The Exercise of Control.* Cambridge, MA: Cambridge University Press.

Breus, M. (2011). *The Sleep Doctor's Diet Plan.* New York, NY: Rodale, Inc.

Dweck, C. S. (2006). *Mindset: The New Psychology of Success.* New York, NY: Random House, Inc.

Epstein, L. J. (2007). *A Good Night's Sleep.* New York, NY: McGraw Hill.

Frankl, V. (1963). *Man's Search for Meaning.* Boston, MA: Beacon Press.

Goldberg, E. (2001). *The Executive Brain: Frontal lobes and the civilized mind.* New York, NY: Oxford University Press.

Goleman, D. (1995). *Emotional Intelligence: Why it can matter more than IQ.* New York, NY: Bantam Books.

Gordon, P. (2004). "Numerical Cognition Without Words: Evidence from Amazonia" Science 15, October 2004: 4496-499. DOI: 10.1126/ science. 1094492.

Hallowell, E. M. (2002). *The childhood roots of happiness: Five steps to help kids create and sustain lifelong joy.* New York, NY: Ballantine Books.

Jacobs, G. D. (1998). *Say Good Night To Insomnia: The 6-week program.* New York, NY: St. Martins Griffin.

Johnson, S. (1998). *Who Moved My Cheese: An A-Mazing Way to Deal with Change in Your Work and in Your Life.* New York, NY: G. P. Putnam's Sons.

LeDoux, J. (1998). *The Emotional Brain: The Mysterious Underpinnings of Emotional Life.* New York, NY: Simon & Schuster, Inc.

Lehrer, J. (2009) *How We Decide.* Boston, MA: Mariner Books, Houghton Mifflin Harcourt.

Lovre, C. (2004). "Workshop on Crisis Intervention, Trauma, and Stress." Crisis Management Institute. Bloomington, IN: National Education Service.

Lupine, S. J. (2004). "The impact of socioeconomic status on children's stress hormone levels, emotional processing, and memory performance." Learning and the Brain Conference. Boston, MA: Public Information Resources.

Mednick, S. C. (2006). *Take a Nap! Change Your Life.* New York, NY: Workman Publishing Company, Inc.

Oliver, B. "Parent to Parent Program." Merritt Island, FL: The Passage Group.

Plaford, G.R. (2006). *Bullying and the Brain: Using Cognitive and Emotional Intelligence to Help Kids Cope.* Lanham, MD: Rowman & Littlefield Education.

Plaford, G. R. (2009). *Sleep and Learning: The Magic that Makes Us Healthy and Smart.* Lanham, MD: Rowman & Littlefield Education.

Restak, R. (2003). *The New Brain: How the Modern Age Is Rewiring Your Mind.* Emmaus, PA: Rodale, Inc.

Robbins, A. (1991). *Awaken the Giant Within: How to take immediate control of your mental, physical & financial destiny!* New York, NY: Firside, Simon & Schuster, Inc.

Santhi, N., et.al. (2011). "The spectral composition of evening light and individual differences in the suspension of melatonin and delay of sleep in humans." The Journal of Pineal Research Sept 20. doi: 10.1111/j. 1600-079X.2011.00970.x.

Schallenberg, E. G. (2004). "Music Lessons Enhance IQ." Psychological Science. August 2004 15: 511-514, doi: 10.1111/j.0956-7976.2004.00711.x

Schultz, W. (1998). "Predictive Reward Signal of Dopamine Neurons." Journal of Neurophysiology 80, 1-27.

Shoda, Y.; Mischel, W.; Peake, P. (1990). "Predicting Adolescent Cognitive and Self-Regulatory Competencies from Preschool Delay of Gratification: Identifying Diagnostic." Developmental Psychology 26 (6): 978-986.

Toffler, A. (1970). *Future Shock.* New York, NY: Random House, Inc.

CPSIA information can be obtained
at www.ICGtesting.com
Printed in the USA
BVHW071139240521
607998BV00004B/363

9 781641 514767